We S
the Re

We Stormed the Reichstag

A War Correspondent Remembers

Vassili J. Subbotin

Translated by Tony Le Tissier

Pen & Sword
MILITARY

Published in German as *Wir stürmten den Reichstag. Aufzeichnungen eines Frontkorrespondenten* by Militärverlag in 1980

First published in Great Britain in 2017 by
PEN & SWORD MILITARY
an imprint of
Pen & Sword Books Ltd
47 Church Street
Barnsley
South Yorkshire
S70 2AS

ISBN 978-1-47387-775-7

Typeset by Concept, Huddersfield HD4 5JL.
Printed and bound in England by CPI Group (UK) Ltd, Croydon CR0 4YY.

Pen & Sword Books Ltd incorporates the imprints of Pen & Sword Archaeology, Atlas, Aviation, Battleground, Discovery, Family History, History, Maritime, Military, Naval, Politics, Railways, Select, Social History, Transport, True Crime, and Claymore Press, Frontline Books, Leo Cooper, Praetorian Press, Remember When, Seaforth Publishing and Wharncliffe.

For a complete list of Pen & Sword titles please contact
PEN & SWORD BOOKS LIMITED
47 Church Street, Barnsley, South Yorkshire, S70 2AS, England
E-mail: enquiries@pen-and-sword.co.uk
Website: www.pen-and-sword.co.uk

Contents

List of Plates

Introduction

Vassili Subbotin's account of his personal experiences during the Second World War, in which he served as a conscript and finally as a commissioned war correspondent on the newspaper of the 150th Idritz Infantry Division, follows this introduction. It was as a result of this role that he eventually became involved in the storming of the Reichstag and post-war managed to regain contact with some of his former colleagues, revisited Berlin and wrote an account of his experiences.

Although the Reichstag building had been severely damaged in an arson attack by a deranged Dutchman on 27 February 1933, it remained of considerable historic significance to the Soviets and became the prime objective in their attack on Berlin. Following the fire, the German parliament had been transferred some 400m across the park in front of the Reichstag to the Kroll Opera House.

Then in January 1938 it was announced that a new plan existed for the transformation of the city, and on the night of the capitulation of France in 1940 Hitler issued the order that the fulfilment of this plan was to be completed by 1950.

My drawing (p. xviii) describing the Soviet attack on the Reichstag shows the stripped and partially cleared Diplomatic Quarter, the adjacent Ministry of the Interior, the large flooded area in the centre marking the proposed new course for the Spree and the ditch for the connecting underground railway to the proposed 'Great Hall' curving south, together with the outlines of temporary construction site buildings opposite the Kroll Opera House and in front of the Reichstag.

It was on the afternoon of 28 April 1945 that the leading elements of the 79th Rifle Corps advancing along the street known as Alt Moabit first caught sight of the Reichstag building through the swirling clouds of smoke and dust that obscured the central districts of the city. The fixation of the Soviets on the Reichstag as their goal was to highlight this particular part of the battle to heroic proportions. Heroic as it undoubtedly was in its execution, this episode also emphasizes the ruthless exploitation of the troops involved and the fundamental military errors made by their commanders in their haste to meet a politically dictated deadline. The pressure from Stalin downwards to get the Red Flag flying from the top of the Reichstag in time for the May Day celebrations was such that no one in the chain of command wanted to be in a position where he could be accused of sabotaging the project. The cost was of no consequence.

The news created great excitement and Corps Commander Major General S.N. Perevertkin hastened forward to see for himself. He decided to establish his command post in the tall Customs building at the end of the street overlooking the Moltke Bridge and the approaches to the Reichstag. The 150th Rifle Division was already beginning to assemble in the vicinity of the Customs building, and he called forward the 171st Rifle Division to assemble in the ruins of the Lehrter Railway Station on the other side of the street.

Immediately to the left was the Schiffahrts Canal denoting the corps boundary, behind which the Germans were still holding out as far north as Invalidenstrasse. There were also German troops north of the Spree on Perevertkin's right in Lehrter Goods Station, which had not been on his line of advance and so remained uncleared. Across his front the river was some 50m wide, the stone quay of the Customs Yard dropping 10ft to the water level in full view of the enemy opposite. The only ready means available for crossing the river was the massive stone-built Moltke Bridge, which was strongly barricaded at either end, ready mined for demolition, strewn with barbed wire and other obstacles, and swept by artillery and machine-gun fire from positions concealed in the buildings on the far bank. Across the bridge on either side of Moltkestrasse were the badly damaged but still standing and heavily fortified buildings of the former Diplomatic Quarter and the Ministry of the Interior. Behind them aerial reconnaissance had revealed the presence of a large flooded pit from which a submerged anti-tank ditch extended right across Königsplatz in front of a series of trenches and gun emplacements connecting with the Reichstag itself. Further artillery and mortars were entrenched in the Tiergarten and the whole area had been mined. Like the other buildings in the area, the Reichstag had its doors and windows bricked up except for small gunports, and was to prove virtually impervious to shelling. All these buildings had street-level cellar windows providing ready-made gun embrasures, and high in the burnt-out frame of the Reichstag dome were hidden further machine-guns.

The large water obstacle, which would influence the line of attack, was in fact part of the cutting intended for the diversion of the Spree to enable the construction of Albert Speer's Great Hall on the north side of the square, the anti-tank ditch being in fact a cutting for a U-Bahn tunnel leading to Moltkestrasse. The tunnel running parallel to Siegesallee had been completed as far north as Königsplatz before work had been abruptly abandoned two or three years previously, leaving the construction site littered with temporary buildings, all of which had been incorporated into the defence system.

The Red Air Force's attacks had to be called off due to the narrowness of the battlefield, but ground-attack aircraft continued to simulate attacks as a deterrent in support of the ground forces. The massed Soviet heavy artillery was now concentrating its efforts on this area between the Spree and the Landwehr Canal, which Chuikov's troops were preparing to cross from the south, and there was no shortage of ammunition.

It was decided to attempt a surprise infantry attack across the Moltke Bridge with a view to establishing a foothold on the near corner of the Diplomatic Quarter on the left, using one battalion from each of the two leading divisions. This could then be expanded into a bridgehead to enable the 150th Rifle Division to launch an attack across Moltkestrasse into the Ministry of the Interior building dominating the crossing point, while the 171st Rifle Division cleared the remainder of the Diplomatic Quarter. Once secured, these buildings would provide a firm base for the attack on the Reichstag itself.

Casualties sustained in the fierce fighting through Alt Moabit had been replaced by released Soviet prisoners of war and the leading battalions were now back up to full strength. A battalion had an establishment of 500 men and consisted of three rifle companies, a support weapons company and a battery of 45mm field guns, but for this operation the battalions were split into two assault groups each, to which were added detachments of armoured self-propelled artillery. Also under the command of the 79 Rifle Corps were the 10th Independent Flame-Thrower Battalion and the 23rd Tank Brigade.

Soviet estimates of the opposition were later quoted as being some 5,000 German troops of various kinds. However, SS Sergeant Major Willi Rogmann, who in addition to commanding the 'Anhalt' Regiment's mortar platoon was also responsible for taking forward troops of rounded-up stragglers to reinforce the regiment's various companies throughout this stage of the battle, reports that an unknown number of Allgemeinde-SS under a police colonel were defending the offices in the Ministry of the Interior, and that only SS Lieutenant

Babick's company of some 100 potential NCOs was deployed between the bridge, the Reichstag and the Brandenburg Gate. As reinforcements, Babick belatedly received about 250 sailors of the 'Grossadmiral Dönitz' Battalion and about 100 Volkssturm. There were also some tanks of the 11th SS 'Hermann von Salza' Tank Battalion in the Tiergarten.

During the evening of 28 April Rogmann went forward to reconnoitre the Molte Bridge area with Sergeant Major Kurt Abicht of a battery commanded by a one-armed artillery lieutenant who, having lost his own unit, had attached himself to Rogmann's platoon with two guns, for which the officer had managed to scrounge some rounds from the Reichs Chancellery. The police colonel refused to allow them to set up an observation post in the Ministry of the Interior building, so they went across the street into the Diplomatic Quarter. Rogmann first tried out some of his rockets on the Customs Yard and Washingtonplatz, causing havoc among the Soviet artillery massing there. Rogmann and Abicht then set up their two mortars and the guns to cover the bridge.

The 79th Rifle Corps' attack across the Moltke Bridge was a daring and bloody affair. Both sides made their preparations during the evening of 28 April. The Soviets then used heavy tanks to push aside the barricade on the northern edge of the bridge, while the Germans reinforced the two 'Anhalt' companies, one on either side of the Ministry of the Interior, with 250 of the sailors that Dönitz had had flown in, and sent forward observers to control the mortar, rocket and artillery fire, all of which weapons were then zeroed in on their respective targets. The rockets caused much confusion among the exposed Soviet artillery based on Washingtonplatz, but no fire was returned.

Then at midnight, the two leading battalions launched their surprise attack across the bridge, unheralded by any artillery barrage, but immediately supported by their artillery firing across the Spree on either side of the bridge at point-blank range. However, the 'Anhalt' was ready for them; the attackers were caught on the wire of the southern barricade in a hail of fire from enfiladed machine-guns and blasted by the gun and mortars directed at the bridge. At the same time, the supporting Soviet artillery was brought under rocket attack from a battery located at Potsdamer Platz, causing considerable disruption.

General Perevertkin then resumed his attack by sending in heavy tanks to push aside the southern barricade. To counter this, the

Germans used the fire of anti-tank guns and some tanks of the 11th SS 'Hermann von Salza' Panzer Battalion located in the Tiergarten, but were then joined by the heavy guns of the zoo flak-tower, the impact of whose shells hurled the tanks aside in an orgy of destruction that blocked the bridge with wreckage.

The Soviet infantry then came forward once more and, with the cover provided by this wreckage, were able to secure a small bridgehead in the near corner of the Diplomatic Quarter. By daybreak the remaining troops of the 150th and 171st Rifle divisions are said to have got across the bridge into this building, from where they began expanding their bridgehead by the usual method of mouse-holing their way through the line of buildings fronting Moltkestrasse, while the 171st Rifle Division cleared the remainder of the block with the 525th Rifle Regiment working the Kronprinzenufer side on the left and the 380th Rifle Regiment in the middle. That so many units were able to cram into such a small space is indicative of the numbers of casualties that must have been sustained in this operation and the determination of the Soviet command.

The SS officials in the Ministry of the Interior building had also joined in the fight, firing machine-guns across Moltkestrasse. Then, as dawn broke, Soviet self-propelled guns and field artillery pieces could be seen firing openly from the Customs Yard. These were engaged with devastating effect by the zoo flak-tower's heavy guns, but the Soviets simply brought in more self-propelled guns and tanks to replace them.

The 'Anhalt' then mounted a counterattack, which unexpectedly combined with another on the northern bank, where a unit of the 9th Parachute Division that had been defending the Lehrter Railway Station and had in the meantime withdrawn to the goods station, suddenly broke through the Soviet lines to cross the bridge, creating havoc on its way and bringing a welcome reinforcement of about 100 men to the defence. The effect on the Soviet bridgehead appears to have been to pin it down temporarily. Further advantage was taken of the ensuing confusion to send forward a demolition team to blow the bridge. Unfortunately the charges proved inadequate for the massive structure and only half of the southernmost of the three central spans fell into the river, still leaving sufficient room for vehicles to pass.

At 0700 hours the next stage of the operation began with a 10-minute barrage as the 150th Rifle Division prepared to cross Moltkestrasse to the main entrance of the Ministry of the Interior, or 'Himmler's House' as they dubbed it. The two middle buildings on the Soviet side of the street had their carriage entrances directly opposite, so one can assume that this was the route taken. The Soviets dashed across the street and flattened themselves against the walls of the Ministry, threw grenades into the doorway and then charged through into the hall beyond. Fighting rapidly spread up the main staircase and along the various floors, and was to last all day amid the choking smoke of fires started on the carpets and furniture littered around. The SS defenders resisted fiercely and eventually the 150th Rifle Division had to call in their second echelon, the 674th Rifle Regiment, to clear the south-western corner of the building.

Between 0830 and 1000 hours there was a massive artillery bombardment of the Reichstag position in an attempt to weaken the defences there for the forthcoming attack, but there was no follow-up, for the attacking divisions were still busy clearing the buildings in their path, as they would be for the rest of the day.

By 0400 hours on the morning of 30 April the 150th Rifle Division had eliminated the German defenders of the Ministry of the Interior and the 171st Rifle Division had finished clearing the western half of the Diplomatic Quarter. The latter's 525 Rifle Regiment was lining Alsenstrasse and there was to be no respite.

The frantic urgency imposed from above can be seen in the way the Soviets launched the next stage of the operation only half an hour later. The decision to push the exhausted soldiers forward without a break, involving a complete change in tactics as they emerged into the open from the buildings they had just taken, and without time for proper reconnaissance or preparation was to prove a costly error. The constant long-range bombardment had not silenced the defence, and the exposed infantry immediately came under a hail of fire, not only from the front and flank as expected, from the Reichstag and Tiergarten, but also from the rear as they wheeled round to face their objective. For the Germans had established a formidable strongpoint in the ruins of the Kroll Opera House with machine-guns and artillery mounted high in the bombed-out structure. Under these circumstances the attack quickly fizzled out.

It was now obvious that the Kroll Opera House would have to be tackled before the attack on the main objective could be developed further, and the 597th and 598th Rifle regiments of the 207th Rifle Division were brought forward for this purpose. However, in order to get to the Kroll Opera House, they had first to clear the buildings standing on the Schlieffenufer, and this would take time.

Meanwhile more support weapons were being brought across the bridge to assist the main attack, all having to run a gauntlet of fire coming from the same Schlieffenufer buildings and the Tiergarten beyond. Tanks, guns and rocket-launchers were brought up, some ninety barrels in all. A number of the guns of the 420th Anti-Tank Artillery Division were placed on the upper floors of the Ministry of the Interior building and ten rocket-launchers set up in the courtyard.

The attack was resumed at 1130 hours with the usual heavy preliminary bombardment, and this time the infantry got as far as the flooded anti-tank ditch. The Germans mounted some local counterattacks, including one of battalion size in Alsenstrasse that the 525th Rifle Regiment managed to beat back.

At 1300 hours the Soviets tried again with a massive barrage from their close-support artillery and tanks, plus many more guns lined up across the river, and even some infantry joined in with captured Panzerfausts. After some 30 minutes of this fire the infantry started forward once more, but were promptly pinned down again with the assistance of the anti-aircraft batteries on the zoo flak-tower. However, on the left flank the 171st Rifle Division managed to clear the eastern half of the Diplomatic Quarter and secured the southern end of the Kronprinzen Bridge against the possibility of a German counterattack from across the river. This progress also enabled the introduction of tanks and self-propelled guns forward of the line of the anti-tank ditch to assist the exposed infantry in front of the Reichstag.

The area that the infantry now had to cross was littered with the temporary structures and other debris of the abandoned works project, among which a series of trenches, barbed wire, mines and a determined enemy presented formidable obstacles for the infantry to overcome, and it was now clear that they would need the cover of darkness for these last 200yds.

Meanwhile at 1425 hours, Major General V.M. Shatilov, commanding the 150th Rifle Division, reported up the chain of command that he thought he had seen a red flag over the steps of the Reichstag near the right-hand column. As the leading battalions contained several dare-devils eager to have a go at planting a flag on the Reichstag, including a group of volunteers from Corps Headquarters under the Commander's aide, Major M.M. Bondar, with the 150 Rifle Regiment and some gunners under Captain V.N. Makov with the 756th, the possibility that someone had gone forward with a flag was not totally unlikely. However, the wild enthusiasm with which this report was received resulted in Marshal G.K. Zhukov issuing his Operation Order No. 06 of that day in which he said: 'Units of the 3rd Shock Army ... having broken the resistance of the enemy, have captured the Reichstag and hoisted our Soviet Flag on it today, April 30th 1945 at 1425 hours'. This erroneous report was flashed on to Moscow and reported abroad, but when the war correspondents and photographers started converging on the Reichstag they found the Soviet troops still only halfway across Königsplatz and pinned down by gunfire.

Clearly painfully aware of this error, according to Captain S.A. Neustroev, Major General Shatilov was now dementedly ordering his troops: 'Somehow you have to hoist a flag or pennant, even on the columns at the main entrance. Somehow!'

The first attempt is said to have been made sometime that day by two groups of pilots of the 115th Air Fighter Regiment, who dropped some 6m-wide red silk panels inscribed with the word *'Pobeda'* ('Victory') on the dome of the building while flying at minimum height and speed.

Eventually it was 1800 hours before the attack could be resumed, but this time, with the close support of their armour, some of the infantry were able to get right up the steps of the Reichstag to the still-intact bricked-up doorways. Fortunately they had two light mortars with them, and by aligning these weapons horizontally were able to blast a small hole in the brickwork and so make their way into the main entrance hall.

In these attacks across the open ground the infantry had been led by their regimental and battalion standards, and the survivors of the leading battalion, which had in fact spearheaded the entire corps' operation through Berlin, took their standard in with them as they began to expand their position within the building. By the time they had established telephone communication with their regimental headquarters, their radios having failed to work indoors, they had already fought their standard up to the second floor. However, the Military Council of the 3rd Shock Army had previously issued special banners, distinguished by extra large hammer and sickle emblems, to each of its nine rifle divisions for such an eventuality, and so the 150th Rifle Division's 'Red Banner No. 5', which had a hand-picked escort of Party and Komsomol members, was hastily despatched with instructions to hoist it on the roof of the Reichstag without delay.

Meanwhile the vicious hand-to-hand fighting was spreading out on the various floors of the building as more and more Soviet troops broke their way in. The Germans put up a stubborn resistance and the Soviets experienced great difficulty trying to find their way in almost total darkness in the unfamiliar surroundings. Eventually, by using small groups to distract attention from their main purpose, two sergeants of the special banner party managed to find their way to the rear of the building, from where a stairway led up to the roof, and there they found a mounted statue and wedged the staff of the banner into a convenient crevice high above the ground. This was officially recorded as having taken place some 70 minutes before midnight and the commencement of May Day in Moscow.

Next day photographs were taken in daylight to commemorate the great event, but the flag was so high that the photographer had Sergeants M.A. Yegorov and M.V. Kantara change places with him, thus producing the famous image of hoisting the flag against the background of the Brandenburg Gate instead of an unidentifiable piece of sky. Although Yegorov and Kantara were both made 'Heroes of the Soviet Union' for their deed, they had in fact failed to meet the deadline, having been soundly trounced by the group of gunners under Captain V.N. Makov, who had voluntarily accompanied the infantry in the attack on the Reichstag and secured their flag on the Goddess of Victory statue that stood high above the front of the building. Captain Makov was able to report their achievement by radio direct to the corps commander. They too had been followed about 10 minutes later by members of Lieutenant Sergei E. Sorokin's reconnaissance platoon, who had also hoisted a flag on the roof, both parties having achieved their aim before midnight and some two to three hours before the official party, but these initiatives were only rewarded by a lesser decoration, the Order of the Red Banner.

Fighting continued inside the Reichstag all day on 1 May. The German defence fought on desperately under the command of SS Lieutenant Babick of the SS 'Anhalt' Regiment, whose command post was located in a cellar across the street at the rear of the building and connected to it by a tunnel. The Reichstag caught fire, adding to the misery of the combatants, for whom there was no water available with which to quench the thirst aroused by the dust and smoke that chocked them. Gradually the upper storeys of the building were cleared, but the defence fought on in the cellars (which also accommodated a hospital) and it was not until General Weidling's order

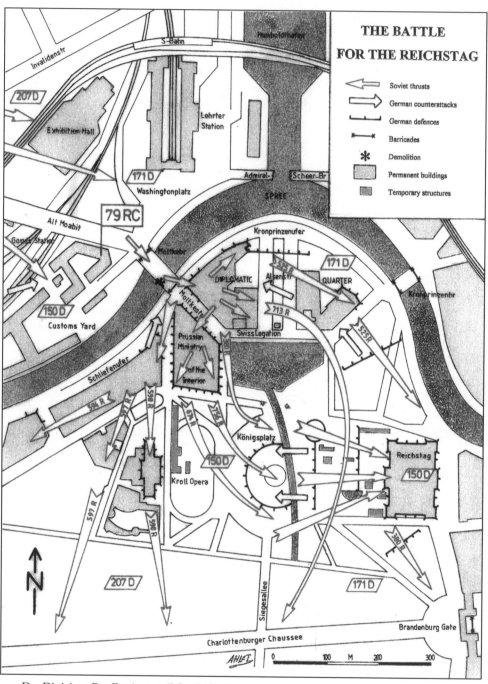

D = Division; R = Regiment; RC = Rifle Corp.

to surrender was received that the survivors laid down their arms at 1300 hours on 2 May.

It seems that both the 674th and 756th Rifle regiments of the 150th Rifle Division actually fought inside the Reichstag and that the 380th Rifle Regiment of the 171st Rifle Division, after having assisted in the storming of the building, re-emerged to secure the Brandenburg Gate corner of the Tiergarten, from where they appear to have penetrated as far as Pariser Platz and the Adlon Hotel. The 171st Rifle Division's two other rifle regiments, the 525th and 713th, secured the river bank and Siegesallee approaches respectively, while the two regiments of the 207th Rifle Division closed up to the Charlottenburger Chausee (now Strasse des 17, Juni) to await the arrival of the 8th Guards Army from the south. In accomplishing this particular mission the 79th Rifle Corps claim to have taken some 2,600 prisoners and counted 2,500 enemy dead, but these numbers exceed the defenders known to have been fielded in this area about tenfold! Their own casualties were not published separately, but significantly the Soviet War Memorial, which was established across the top of the adjacent Siegesallee shortly afterwards, has 2,200 of their dead buried in its grounds.

CHAPTER ONE

Breaking Through to the Oder

The soldiers marched, their eyes fixed on the heavens. They marched along looking at the sun. A large rainbow-coloured circle accompanied it. The soldiers with a slung rifle or submachine-gun looked up at the sky astonished and puzzled. They had never seen such a sun before. It stood high in the sky. Since morning it had been unbearably hot.

The soldiers marched along roads, tracks and across fields, everyone looking up as if bewitched. The orange-coloured, unusually large disk was shedding only a little light. An unnatural twilight spread and in the distance the smoke covered the ball of fire of the gleaming circle. The sun had risen, glowing fire red on the horizon, and then the light had gone pale in a rare natural display.

The soldiers looked steadfastly at this haze-covered sun without hurting their eyes as it was as if they were looking through sooty glass. So they marched on, taking care not to lose step.

*　*　*

Do you know how one feels when one goes into the attack for the first time? Generally speaking going into the attack is the same, whether for the first, second or third time. I will try to explain it to you. Are you already at a great height? Have you looked down from a roof or the window of a ten-storey building? Have you perhaps jumped off a tower with a parachute?

It is just about the same feeling.

I will never forget my first jump. I was still a child. In those days every child had had to have jumped at least once – it was the fashion. I climbed up the jump tower and went onto the plank, the parachute hanging over me, fastened to my body by straps. I knew that I could not fall, the parachute would hold me, but my knees were weak and I was in low spirits. I struggled for breath, which came with a whistling sound. My stomach had a queasy feeling.

One is just the same when the order comes to go into the attack, as one climbs out of the trench and the machine-guns rattle and one plunges into the turmoil.

Just like jumping with a parachute, but much more aggravating.

But in 1941, when I first had to go into the attack, I found it quite easy. Presumably because I was still young and was not the first. However the memory of it left a deep impression on me.

Today I don't need to charge out any more. I can stay in the trench.

The soldiers, silent, pale as if stunned by their experiences – there had been a tank attack – move aside, giving me room to go past.

There are not many of them. I watch them get ready, laying hand grenades on the breastworks and brushing aside the earth in their way. And they are silent.

And yesterday? What happened yesterday, and how did I get into this trench?

I was dead tired and I had wrapped myself in a tent cloth in a trench on the banks of the Oder not far from the water. I had immediately fallen asleep. My ears were accustomed to the roaring of the artillery and the rolling of the tanks, and so I was not woken up by them.

Yesterday our people broke through the front, and I had slept through the beginning of the offensive on the Oder. The artillery preparation had been overwhelming, it was said, and the searchlights had covered everything in blinding light. But I had been asleep.

What is wrong with me? It has already happened to me once before. We were lying in a wood, surrounded and fired on by mortars. There was a frightful din. We had dug trenches and lined and camouflaged them with pine leaves. The firing went on all night. It was so dark that one could not see one's hand in front of one's face. And we all slept. When we woke up we saw that the wood had been shot to pieces. The trees around us were in splinters.

I am only tired, or is it a reaction to long-term stress?

* * *

It is extraordinary to imagine that as a young man, only a few years over 20, I was sitting in a trench on the Oder.

The day before yesterday I had woken up in a building near the front line. All were still asleep. It was thundering around us and the building was shaking.

The situation was immediately obvious to me. The offensive had begun and I had to get out. I needed no order for this. In no time at all I was dressed, threw my bag over my shoulder, shook the man who was sleeping alongside me in the bed and told him I was going.

I did not have to look for the way. I simply went in the direction of the explosions going over us. The day was already dawning. The sun came up as I crossed over the Oder on a swaying bridge lying half under water.

The morning made me happy and not only because I was well rested and the air tasted so fresh. It is starting at last! I am only annoyed that no one has told me exactly when. It seems it was not necessary to tell us, the workers on the divisional newspaper. All must have been known the evening before, but no one had informed us.

The bridgehead was just beyond the Oder in a torn-up, deformed hollow. I had been shown the bridgehead from the bank of the dam on this side. Everything was clear to me and appeared extensive. But I had hardly got into the disrupted maze of trenches than I lost my orientation and was unable to find my way. I went here and there until I realized that I had been wrong and it was not so easy to find a place that I had seen so clearly from the dam as if on a map.

Finally I managed to find the well-camouflaged position of our mortars. The battery commander and a platoon commander were brothers, both quiet and taciturn soldiers. One was called Anatoli, the other Grigori. One had to know them well to tell them apart.

Anatoli was delighted. 'It is you?' he asked as I climbed into the dugout. He was sitting bent over as the dugout was low. One could not dig deep because of the water level.

That morning I wandered for a long time through trenches unknown to me that ran left and right. When a trench ended I climbed up and went on until I landed in a new one.

The air was fresh and damp. I was wearing a waterproof over my uniform. It was spring, the second half of April, but this year we had put on the summer uniforms. I had already exchanged my lamb's wool cap for a peaked one, so I walked around the bridgehead, the sun high in the sky.

Looking for information and my friends I came through fighting positions and observation posts, meeting gunners and infantrymen. I also looked in on the rear services. Unexpectedly I came across a general in a trench section. He stood there with binoculars to his eyes. He looked at me briefly. There was thick black hair under his cap. He was young.

I did not quite recognize him, perhaps because he was had camouflage over his cap and because he was wearing a dark uniform jacket. He was the corps commander.

I did not report to him, not wanting to introduce myself. The general appeared not to have expected it either, and silently put the binoculars back to his eyes. I went on.

I kept on losing my way between the water-filled trenches. They were really too shallow to provide shelter. Then I came to a dugout. The entrance was badly covered with a mud-smeared tent-half. Curiously, I looked within.

Inside sat a regimental commander, a tall, gaunt lieutenant colonel. He was crouching down in order to avoid hitting the cover with his head. Apart from him there were another two soldiers in the shelter, a radio operator and a girl from the medical post or the field kitchen.

I had not arrived at a convenient moment. The lieutenant colonel with a pipe pressed in his fist, was shouting: 'Wait, wait a minute!' Suddenly he raised his voice: 'How many? Say it calmly! Where? Right, left? – Thirty-two?'

Tanks were attacking over there.

The lieutenant colonel forced himself to calm down before he replied: 'Thirty-two tanks, that was nothing trivial!'

There was a pause. Then we heard a voice coming from the receiver reporting: 'Not thirty-two, but four.'

'Thank goodness,' said the commander. 'Eight times less!' And he laughed.

I asked him the way to the battalion. His sergeant major was supposed to be going there, but he was not available at the moment. I should make my way to the Komsomol organizer, who knew the way. I found him in a trench near the regimental commander's dugout. He was asleep.

When I woke him he looked at me in an unfriendly manner and began wrapping his footcloths.

'What are you doing here?' I asked him, immediately realizing that I had no right to ask this question.

'I have to remove the dead', he answered and went on to say that he had had no sleep the whole night.

We set off. 'It is quite close,' he said.

We went along a trench. Where it ended we had to go across an open field. There were heights on the left-hand side. The bullets whistled strongly. We could not go along upright. My escort did not know the way, losing his sense of direction. It was obvious to me that we had come out on the river bank. I told him so. He contradicted me, justifying himself, and talking so much that in the end I did not know whether he really knew the way or not.

We came to a water ditch, a kind of canal. We had no wish to climb into the cold spring water, especially as we did not know how deep it was. Perhaps it would come up to our necks, perhaps we would be unable to touch the bottom. So we walked along the waterside on the foot-wide path under the bushes, careful not to slip off. We stopped often to take a breath.

It was a difficult task not to fall in the water and not to raise our heads too high. As soon as our heads were seen above the bushes, a machine-gun would rattle.

Then we were standing in front of a wire fence. It came up out of the water to the embankment. We had to go through whether we wanted to or not.

We discovered a hole in the barrier, large enough for a man to get through. The wires were swinging dangerously in the wind. Near the hole was a dead soldier, one of ours. We recognized him by his wadded jacket.

We had to get through. We had to get through the wire, without getting stuck in it, and without being hit by a bullet. We looked at the fallen man only three steps away.

The Komsomol organizer advised me not to follow close behind him. And in fact, he had hardly got through the fence when the machine-gun started rattling away again.

The Komsomol organizer had made it through unscathed and had immediately pressed himself to the ground. Would it go the same for me? I waited a while and then jumped up.

Damn it! I had got stuck, my coat was caught on the wire. What I had feared most had occurred. I tugged strongly on the coat and ripped it loose. I was free.

I had hardly got under cover when the machine-gun renewed its firing.

'Still, stay still! Don't talk so loud, the Germans are right close!'

I had already discovered Tverdochleb, the battalion commander, a large, somewhat clumsy man. Only a few soldiers were in the trench.

'Were you abandoned by the battalion?' The deputy battalion commander, a small dark-haired, no longer young man, walked up to me.

I pulled out my notebook. I had found it somewhere. It was bound in artificial red leather and there was a word in a foreign language on the first page that I could not decipher.

The battalion commander laughed in astonishment. He apparently did not understand why I had pushed my way forward to him. He had taken two trenches and a village alone that day, and his battalion now only consisted of about fifteen men.

They surrounded me, clearly pleased that someone had got through to them, and someone from the press, a reporter. All appeared to have regarded themselves as having been damned, thrown into the break-through and then forgotten.

They spoke quietly, but one interrupted the other. Everyone wanted to show me the tank that they had shot up shortly before. It was still smoking.

The soldiers looked cautiously over the parapet. They did not want to place themselves in danger unnecessarily. Only new boys, inexperienced soldiers, go into places where there is no need. I knew these lads. If they are in a forward position for the first time they think there is no danger when everything is so still and quiet. But it is only quiet because the experienced soldiers that know the front hold themselves back not wanting to invite danger.

I made a lot of notes. I wanted to write down every word that they said. They all listened intently as the battalion commander told his story, especially those standing further away, such as a black-haired lieutenant with an impressively intelligent face.

I found it difficult to make out among the soldiers in this trench, only a few metres distant from the Germans, who was a hero about whom it would be worth writing. In my eyes they were all heroes.

Then I had to go back. It was already getting dark.

We went back the same way that we had come. Under the fence lay a sapper cutting the wire with shears. An invisible machine-gun was still firing from the flank, but the bullets whistled away over the fence.

The dead man had been removed.

We continued along the foot-wide track, being careful not to make a noise.

* * *

1943. The horse trotted along happily, swinging its tail. The driver – I could not see his face – only tugged at the reins if the horse lost its step. That was enough. The winter night was quiet and mild. It was snowing. The flakes fell on my face, my cheeks and eyes. They melted under my breath. My chin and collar were moist.

It was only snowing a little. The way remained passable. It was not a road, rather a track, but polished smooth and well used. And the horse was strong and lively.

I was wearing leather boots. I had not yet been issued with felt boots, but I was covered with a half pelt and had pelt gloves. The old driver – what a good man I had stumbled across – had also covered my legs with straw. I was not freezing.

Although I was going to a unit as a front correspondent for the first time and did not know what to expect, I was writing. The unusually mild night and the lightly falling snow wanted me awake. I wrote and my verses said nothing of war.

Villages lay around, but no lights burned. We had liberated these places only shortly before. They were devastated and life had not yet returned, many of the houses having been burnt down to the ground. The inhabitants huddled somehow in the woods in earthen huts. Children were born, but there was no place where they could be registered.

We drove through deserted villages, over fields, and through woods. The land was hilly. Flares rose up and died out. They seemed to me like sheet-lightning.

The track wound its way between the hillocks. I could not see them, but the horse trotted through.

And then we had reached our destination. We stopped at the foot of a hillock. A pale white flare went up and went out again. Something rumbled from time to time nearby. A machine-gun rattled. After a few bursts it was silent again.

Right in front of our noses a door was opened. Someone came out and said something. My companion replied. I clumsily climbed out of the sledge, noticing for the first time that my legs were asleep. I stooped down and entered the bunker.

Immediately the warmth embraced me like in a bath. It was dark in the first room, but a light was burning in the one behind it. A lamp fashioned from a shell case was shedding it, and the warmth pressed upon me from there. The stove consisted of a piece of pipe.

I introduced myself. I had only arrived in the division a few days ago and was still unknown.

The company commander, a lieutenant, was a bit strange. He spoke precisely and thoughtfully, but he was a bit of a joker. 'Orderly, go and tell the Fascist that he should stop ...'.

The firing actually died down. The enemy had been nervous for two days now, someone told me. Obviously he intended something.

The lieutenant was quiet for a while and listened to whether the shots were getting close. Then he came across to us: 'There has to be some relaxation, shall we have a smoke?'

We tore a piece from the newspaper that was covering the table and rolled our cigarettes.

Shortly afterwards it became quiet outside. The enemy had stopped firing.

The lieutenant took the pistol from the table and looked at an officer, apparently a platoon commander, and said: 'So Lieutenant, let us take the opportunity of checking your position.'

When they returned I was already asleep.

A shell had landed close by they said. But all had gone well, only a horse having been wounded. A rear services unit had also dug into this hill. There was even a stable.

I opened my eyes again. In the dull light of the smoky lamp I saw the spruce planks with their rough bark over me. I had woken late. The company commander was not there. I quickly ate from a can of marinated fish, and then went out.

The trench began at the bunker door. It led in a depression through fields and further hillocks. But it was not the trench that drew my attention, but the low barbed wire, which served like a garden fence, a harmless picture at first glance.

A thin layer of snow lay around strewn with small pieces of coal. There were no shell holes to be seen. The earth was frozen hard and the shells were not penetrating to any depth. But I saw a large bomb crater a few metres off the path. It had long since filled with water now covered with a thick layer of ice. The surroundings reminded me of a mining settlement in the north where I had lived years ago. There the snow had mixed with the coal dust and was wide spread over the land.

I saw chimneys some distance away, the remains of villages. And everywhere dugouts, trenches in every hillock, in every depression. I even saw the trenches running in the distance as far as I could see. On the side facing the enemy the soldiers had shovelled red clay or sand on the parapet. And parallel to this, a stone's throw away, stretched another trench, the enemy's.

Instinctively I thought of railway lines, so symmetrical was the distance between the two trenches. Whenever one made a sharp bend, the other followed suit. Only at one place did they go sharply apart as though one had stabbed at the other. This was the first time that I had seen something like this.

I recalled how our tanks had been dug in on the first day of the war. There was no fuel and we had been broken up into small groups, largely concerned with staying away from the main roads. When night fell we hastily dug foxholes in the wood, my sergeant major and I digging together. Not trenches like here, but rather holes. And the next day we had abandoned them. We had dug them during the night only to find shelter should the Fascists attack us, but they had gone past us.

We had no idea where the Fascists were. We came out of one encirclement and went into another. The war had begun for me on the western frontier. I was now one of the few of our regiment still alive, one of the 1921 intake. When the war began I was about 20 years old.

On 22 June we were lying in the barracks on the outskirts of Brody when in the early hours of the morning the duty NCO hauled us out of our beds with 'Alarm!'

Sleepily we wrapped our footcloths, took up our gas masks, unable to understand why we had been woken up so early, especially on a Sunday when alarms were simply never given.

But as I stormed out of the barracks – I was the company commander's runner – I heard the sound of machine-guns rattling. As I raised my head I saw an aircraft flying low over the barracks roof. No, at first I saw only the shadow passing over the roof and then the aircraft. Its markings meant nothing to me because they were unusual.

Towards evening we dug out the pits for our tanks. They had been standing on rollers, the tracks lying well greased under the covering, the machine-guns dismantled and thickly greased somewhere in the barracks.

I recalled it now in 1943. One-and-half years later I was back at the front in the forward positions. It was the same as usual and how quiet with the guns and machine-guns silent. Were we really at the front?

Suddenly there was a shot. A soldier had been shot in the Fascist trenches. The commander of one of our batteries had grabbed a rifle.

That had been 1941.

*   *   *

Smoke, dust and soot, with the sun hiding behind. We were marching, the Oder bridgehead long since behind us. An unnatural light shone over the fields as if in an eclipse. Should it have rained it would have been like an erupting volcano raining earth and ashes.

On the first day we advanced 11km. On the second day there was a hold-up. Then the roaring started off again.

When our offensive began we were lying near Küstrin, which our division had reached about two weeks earlier. We were quartered in a small house on the edge of the town. A pine wood began in front of the house and if one went through it one came to the town. There were still the remains of snow lying in the wood.

The day was grey and monotonous. We were lying on the Oder, but we still had not seen it. Our division was practising overcoming water obstacles at a lake in the woods.

There were contradictory rumours. One said that our people were already standing on the river bank, but another maintained that we were already on the other side and had erected a bridgehead.

Once I climbed up the bell tower of a church, from where I could see the Oder behind the treetops. I admit that my knees were shaking as I stood on the tower and looked around. It was the long forgotten feeling of heights.

Then we moved our position up to the Oder. The Oder here was very wide. It had spread over the banks and flooded the meadows.

* * *

We were waiting here on the Oder until our vehicle could drive across, and I was standing on a rocking, swaying bridge built by the sappers. We were all excited and inspired by the stream of people crossing over the Oder. It was as if I was drunk, standing on the swaying bridge and distributing our newspaper. I shouted, complained without reason and was as happy as everyone. It was a memorable morning.

Two hours later I was standing on the running board and recalled how I had been summoned by Twerdochleb to the editor's office, where they had looked at me with astonishment and in some shock, and I had not quite understood why. They had not expected me. They thought that I had been killed.

Then we crossed the Oder in our vehicle, the pontoon sinking into the water. The vehicle was pitching and shaking, and I held on fast with both hands to the door of the driver's cabin. Mitya, the driver, wanted me to show him the way, which was why I was standing on the running board, otherwise I would have had to sit in the loading bay at the back. I felt much better on the running board, at least I could breath here. In the back only dust came through the gaps in the body.

Trenches ... dugouts.

The ground was churned up, but no barbed wire, none of the concrete defensive walls that we had been told about, and no anti-tank ditches. Such things did not exist here.

We drove along a raised track and came to a building that was burning brightly. I saw the first German soldiers 3 or even 4km beyond the Oder. They were not lying in trenches, but on the bank. They were dead.

We drove on for a long time, rolling over field tracks and slopes over early grass that was trampled, short and bristly. The slopes were overgrown with birds-tares and dried weeds like the hills in our homeland.

And then the sun came up blood red behind us as if it was on fire. We turned into a track that appeared to have been opened only a few days before. We had already been driving for an hour as if lost in this incredible dust, recognizing our own people only with difficulty.

Somebody called out from up ahead. It transpired that the vehicle in front of us was the field post office. I was given a letter. Was it from my sister or from home? I ripped open the envelope right there on the running board, but could not read it with everything swimming before my eyes.

One page was unwritten, but there was the imprint of a child's hand on it. It looked like a maple leaf. It was the imprint of my little daughter's hand.

Towards evening we reached a village, but did not stop. We had lost contact with our own people and had to hurry. We drove up a hill and crossed a little river. All seemed to be in order, then I heard the bridge flooring rattle. I was still standing on the running board and looking at the clouds of dust rising from the way ahead where I should have been looking.

Then suddenly legs hit me in the head. At first I sensed only the blow, and only then the hanging legs. I saw neither a face nor anything else. I only saw the legs of a soldier. He has hanging from a noose over the bridge. They were the legs of a German soldier, the legs of a hanged man. The Fascists had hung him.

* * *

Not everyone knows that in the war of 1812 a similar vehicle was to be encountered on the roads, a carriage packed to the top. It was a field printing shop in which reports and orders were printed and also pamphlets with appeals to the soldiers of the French army. It was the first military printing shop in the field. Vassili Andreyevitch Shukovski drove around with this equipment, he was a famous poet and singer in the Russian army soldiers' camp.

Our army, divisional and front editorial staff went about the roads of war in the trail of our troops with young poets, young journalists just as before. The editing of our divisional newspaper, the newspaper of the 150th Idriz Division, consisted like all other publication units of a wagon, a *kibitka* in the form of a one-and-a-half–tonner. The newspaper was called *Homeland Soldier*. Yes, I admit, we were poets and loved poetry.

I was the youngest in the publishing team and was described as a literary assistant. But I and my comrades in other divisions did not like this description. Assistants are people who work in offices. We called ourselves divisional correspondents, correspondents of the divisional newspaper. In our opinion this expressed our function better.

For our printer – he was also team leader – I was almost a hero, one who was always in the fire. In the eyes of a platoon commander however, I was just an odd ball who visited him in the trenches once a week.

For an outsider this outfit was as colourful as a gypsy encampment. The whole establishment was in the back of the wooden one-and-a-half-tonner – the printer's cases, paper, with printer's black flecked coats and padded jackets, rucksacks and finally ourselves – two typesetters, the printer, the editor, his deputy, the secretary and myself – the literary assistant.

The newspaper was two pages and little larger than a sheet of writing paper. It appeared every other day.

Correspondent of a divisional newspaper – that was hardly a rank. That was a creature that no one understood, however one that understood himself.

Mainly the correspondent moved around. That was his job. Day after day he went around collecting material. Sometimes he returned to the office on the evening of the same day, but mainly he spent the night wherever the night caught up with him. Usually he did not sleep while away, preferring to write.

Today he was in this battalion, tomorrow in another. He went to and fro between the forward positions and the field printing shop. Like a shuttlecock, he dashed here and there. Should a battalion be left out of the order of battle, he went to the new one to find out all about it.

The correspondent has to write everything; information about the fighting and reports on fighting experiences. Today he writes about the machine-gunners, tomorrow about the gunners, next day about the mortar men. Apart from that he must be able to compose rhyming headings, sketches and write accounts. It is good when he is able to draw.

I cut our newspaper masthead out of a piece of linoleum. The old block was so worn out that we could no longer use it. The new one lasted up to Berlin. The correspondent even had to contribute humorous headings.

On hot, sultry days we raised dust on the roads and when it was cold we squeezed between vehicles and marching columns, in the snow and on the country roads.

Often we had to use our own strength to get our vehicle moving. Mitya opened the door for us and we jumped out of the back of the truck.

We delivered a lot and drove a lot. But there was sometimes a quiet moment. We did not waste time, but wrote. We sat there scribbling in our notebooks until late at night and within a short while there was a stack of contributions.

Sometimes we huddled in dugouts, even in German ones. And then we reconnoitred all the routes to the regiments.

This reconnaissance made the divisional correspondents' job difficult. Every time it was from a different perspective; from the division to a regiment, from the regiment to a battalion, and from the battalion to a company, then to a platoon or section, to a forward fighting position or to an observation post.

The correspondent was no colonel. Not even a platoon commander. He had no subordinates and no runner at his disposal. He always went alone. He could count himself lucky if he encountered a medical orderly or a driver carrying ammunition on the way.

There was always the danger of falling into German hands and this thought never left me. They could not have found a better prisoner. On my hips always hung a map case filled with notebooks and writing pads together with the unit locations marked on the accompanying map. And the notebooks contained the whole command structure of the division, including names. My hair stands on end when I think about it.

Once I almost went into an enemy position when I failed to notice the barbed wire. Another time, in winter, I went into the back of a

German gun, but was able to slip away unnoticed. Fortunately I had heard the Germans talking. A third time, this being in summer, I had to throw myself off a hillock to avoid a bombardment. One could well have supposed that I had been leading a company in an attack right over this hill.

As I was making my way along a trench a shell exploded right in front of my eyes and shook me up. I jumped out of the trench and like a hare I ran away under fire.

Once I saw how the Fascists attacked a hill. Right and left in front of me soldiers jumped up out of the trenches, their captain blowing in my ear with his whistle. The soldiers filed through a swamp and threw themselves down in it several times. They took the hill, but were thrown off again within half an hour.

I saw many examples of heroism, of plain, real heroism, generosity, self-sacrifice and patience in overcoming difficulties.

In the winter of 1943/44 in the area of Kalinin the following occurred in our division. In an attack a junior sergeant, the Tartar Saitgalin, lay down while under fire on barbed wire and let the soldiers of his detachment scramble over him like a bridge. I saw this myself.

Upon my return to the field printing shop I went to the regimental headquarters and told the deputy of this act of heroism. 'Why don't you write about it since you were a witness?' the lieutenant colonel said discontentedly.

'But I have already done it', I said. I had immediately sat down and described the whole thing. But the draft lay two weeks with the printers before it appeared first in the army and then in the divisional newspaper.

Our articles were undersigned with the names of the soldiers and sergeants, sometimes even of officers. We had enough material as there were many heroes. In an emergency our driver Mitya Kulikov had to step in. He was a junior sergeant, so we often put 'Junior Sergeant D. Kulikov' under the report.

'Mitya, can I put your name underneath?'

Mitya, who was usually lying under the vehicle, would call out: 'Alright, Comrade Lieutenant!'

Of the nine divisional correspondents that worked in our army's divisions, young lads like myself, almost all of whom wrote poetry, only a few are still alive. Three of them fell and two were badly wounded.

We met sometimes on the tracks coming from the front and cross-ings leading to our units. We had much in common and resembled each other: lean, blackened by wind and frost, in dirty half pelts, with camouflage cloaks and map cases. We did not always carry our pistols with us.

*   *   **

Yesterday was warm and dry. Today it is raining and a cold wind is sweeping over the land.

We concern ourselves with keeping warm while marching, but everything that we are wearing – overcoat and padded jacket – is long since soaked through and we are freezing.

Two days ago we marched off with heads held high, looking up at the sun. Now we look at the road and watch out for the puddles. I was one of those marching, one of a million that had broken out at the Oder, a drop in a storm. The road was roughed up from the tanks. Our coats were soaked full of water, and damp.

I was wearing a long coat with a narrow belt at the back and big lapels. I did not like it. I had had it for a long time already, since Tschelyabinsk, where it was given to me in the reserve regiment when I was allocated to it after coming out of hospital in the winter of 1942. Previously I had only had the uniform of a tank soldier, a jacket of strong waterproof material. I could not forget my old jacket. In 1941 I had made the whole withdrawal in it. I recall that our feet then in 1941 were torn and bleeding. Many had removed their boots and were walking barefoot. We were already on our way for the fifth day. On my left arm was a big red star. I was deputy to the company's political officer.

On the big highway I saw the mass of retreating troops, how some of them shot themselves because they did not want to be left behind but had no strength with which to continue and were unable to climb on means of transport. We were putting many kilometres behind us every day. I had no rifle and helped a soldier, carrying his rifle from time to time. It would be terrible to stay behind and become a prisoner of war.

We were on our way for the fifth day and we had no field kitchen with us. An observer would have taken us for defeated soldiers. That is how we looked, although we had not taken part in any proper fighting. We had no kitchen and no rear services.

Before we emerged from the wood near Podgaizy, where we had spent the night, making our way to Tarnopol, we had had our rusks, two pieces each, nothing since then. Numerous other soldiers had passed through the small Ukrainian villages before us. When an old woman brought out a jug of milk, we all fell on her. It would have been better for her not to have brought anything out.

We approached Tarnopol and thought that it was the end of our march. We thought that we would stay here, that there would be not only fighting, but also rest and that the kitchens would come later.

We hoped. I don't know why.

We could see that the street was on fire. The Germans were already there and we turned off immediately to the east. After that we went over red-hot roads, fields and roads blocked with vehicles. And the roughed-up, bronze-coloured wheat rocked under the heavy, overripe corn. There were trucks lying in the ditches on both sides of the road, abandoned carts and dead people. Again and again came the cry 'Aircraft!' and we ran off.

This went on for five days. Even on the previous nights we had marched without a rest. We had hoped to reach Shepetovka. The whole previous night lights had been burning and we had taken them for those of Shepetovka and had marched towards them. Shepetovka was a place on the old border, the only border town that we knew, and we had marched and marched towards the enticing lights. We pressed on to the old border, where we hoped fortifications must have been built. Quite obviously we would not be going on further, as we would not be falling further back than the old border. We knew that! The battle would take place there.

As day broke the lights vanished and I do not know to this day what those lights were.

At midday we came to the river which separated two towns, Volotshisk and Podvolotshisk.

Near me was a tall captain. He had buckled his belt tight and the Order of the Red Star was resplendent on his clean uniform jacket. This decoration was rare at this time. We looked longingly at it when we encountered someone wearing it.

The captain had the appearance of having participated in the winter war against Finland, which had already come to an end. From time to time he looked at me from the side. He was slim and slender, looking like a boy, and I tried to get closer to him. Whenever I was left behind I tried with all my strength to catch up.

Certainly he as was as robust as I was.

'I wonder,' he said to me once, looking at me half pityingly, half smiling, 'I wonder where you get the strength from. I fall behind, but you go on and on!'

I had no strength. Where would I have got it from? Apart from this I had not eaten anything for four or five days. I just had to maintain the idea of going on like all of us.

The Fascists had closed in on us from left and right, and were always in front of us. We felt that we were surrounded.

On the fifth day I arrived in Proskurov. Yes, it was good in Proskurov. At last my sergeant major and I got something to eat in this town. Each of us got a fresh white loaf. I held mine pressed to my breast like a baby.

But then it began to rain before Proskurov, also then before Kamenez, Podolsk, Volotshisk and Podvolotshisk, as we turned away from Tarnopol and went through the sunken wheat. I had to put on my jacket which I had had slung over my shoulders. I had nothing else, neither a haversack nor a weapon.

To the amazement of the captain, I took a rusk out of my pocket. I too was surprised. The captain looked at me as if I were a magician. A rusk in my pocket, and almost dying of hunger! Apparently it had been in my pocket for a long time, already a very long time. I shared it with the captain. How light the jacket had been in contrast to the water-soaked coat that I am wearing now.

So we distanced ourselves from the Oder this way, marching and avoiding the puddles. We could not sit down or take a rest.

It did not look as if the weather would improve. The sky hung low over us and the neighbourhood was soon covered in clouds and smoke. With short intervals it had rained all through the night. We had occupied quarters in a farm. In the morning I saw prisoners not far from the house. Adolescents! How few of them had coats, and how thin their necks rose out of their collars! They had not grown up yet, but the Fascists had thrown them against our tanks.

A cold wind mingled with rain and we had no rest all day.

The soldiers had tucked their coat tails under their webbing. The sight of soldiers with shortened coats is amusing. Women washing their dirty linen in a stream tuck up their skirts like this.

And it rained and rained. The heavens loomed low around. We marched over fields, tracks and roads. There was mud and water everywhere.

It was easier marching with shortened coats. If one did not lift the coat tails up, they hit against our legs like wooden sticks. However this way they pick up the mud splashes that would otherwise cover our boots and trousers.

Suddenly there was a low-flying aircraft over the column, but no one took cover. The column marched on unperturbed and I thought that it was one of our aircraft, but then through the rain two rockets flew up to the aircraft, one red and one blue. It was a reconnaissance aircraft!

Aircraft seldom flew past and as a rule they were ours, the pilots waving to us.

Shortly before Berlin we saw the Allied squadrons at a great height. We marched on.

There were soldiers wherever one looked. The column had stretched out widely, the soldiers no longer marching in ranks but in single file on either side of the road.

The weapons were getting ever heavier. We climbed down into a depression. A stream flowed through and we waded through it. At the end of the depression we suddenly stood before a grave next to a tank. There was a German trench with its breastwork facing us 2m further on. The tank was one of ours, a tank of English make, and next to this burnt-out tank was a mound of earth with a plank that had the following inscription burnt on it: 'I was one of the first in the attack on Berlin.'

No one told us, but we sensed that Berlin was not far off. I had no idea where it lay.

There was no smoke to be seen, no chimney, no building, nothing but fields and overgrown tracks, no railway lines, nothing. But we were firmly convinced that we were getting nearer and nearer to the city.

The telegraph poles and the pylons of the cross-country services increased, getting closer together, coming from different directions all into one, and we followed these poles like signposts. And one day a wood of towers appeared out of the rain. It was like a vision with towers whose tops were lost in the clouds. Transmission towers. Berlin was close.

CHAPTER TWO

The Track

We drove quickly through the pitch-black night. Snowflakes were dancing in the headlights. A snowstorm was falling. We were standing on the loading platform, with the necks of our half furs pushed up. We were being shuttled here and there, the frozen ice crunching under the wheels.

I could no longer remember whether light was to be seen in the surroundings. The villages were silent. Only the outlines of hillocks were vaguely recognizable. We drove and drove between snow-covered fields, prepared to join the stars on this slippery track, full of pleasure at the fast journey.

Suddenly there was a crack and the truck bumped over an obstacle. The driver pulled over the steering wheel. As we turned we saw two rockets going up.

Machine-guns began to rattle. Our machine-gun on the truck responded.

A moment later we came to a stop. We had lost our way! We were only a hair's breadth from landing in an enemy trench.

Our truck had hit a mine and only through the quick reaction of the driver remained undamaged. We were shocked to the core as the driver took us back safely, complaining about our youthfulness and lack of experience.

I have not forgotten to this day how the trench cut across our way. When I close my eyes I can see it before me. A track, a normal straight track across the fields leading somewhere, suddenly torn up like a barricade.

Beyond it the front of the foremost lines with their rusting barbed wire.

Since then my memory of the war is this route cut off, blocked by a trench.

CHAPTER THREE

The Grey Building

As day broke everyone inside Himmler's House – the Ministry of the Interior – was at the windows. They wanted to see the Reichstag, but a bulky grey building blocked the view.

Battalion commander Neustroyev stood at a cellar window and also looked out. To the right stood trees, to the left extended a ditch, bare and black. It smelt of spring and last year's wilting leaves. The fog had not yet dispersed. The roof was dripping. Neustroyev saw a square, squat building behind the trees. It did not seem to him to be very big. Indeed it had a dome and turrets, but did not appear to be anything special.

The soldiers pressing towards it were convinced. The Reichstag must be here somewhere, but where?

Another battalion commander, Davydov, said that one would only see badly from the cellar. The view was better upstairs.

They climbed up two storeys and looked out. Fog was still rising from the Spree. The Tiergarten lay desolate over there. It was still. They looked at a square that had been torn up by trenches. They saw tanks deep in the park, self-propelled guns and also advertising pillars. There was a river there. Or was it a canal? The building with the dome and turrets looked more imposing from here.

A messenger arrived. Neustroyev was wanted on the telephone. He quickly climbed down to the cellar. Divisional commander Shatilov wanted to know why he was not attacking.

'Comrade Seventy-Seven! The grey building is in my way.'

'Wait a moment ... what sort of building?'

'Right in front of us. I will have to go round it.'

Neustroyev on the telephone in the cellar and the divisional commander in his observation post in Alt Moabit bent over their maps.

Regimental Commander Sintshenko entered the cellar. He had established his staff behind the river, right next to the Swiss Embassy.

'What is in your way? Give me the map!

They rolled it up and passed it over.

Moltke Bridge ... Spree ... Ministry of the Interior ...

'Neustroyev! But that is the Reichstag!'

The battalion commander had not believed it possible that the square, grey building so near to his window was the Reichstag. He thought that the building lay much further away.

Neustroyev's astonishment was understandable. The way to Berlin had been a long one!

Samsonov, a battalion commander in another division, thought the same. 'And then the Reichstag lay before us. We did not believe it at first glance', Samsonov told me many years later in the Army Club in Moscow.

That could be the Reichstag, but is it the right one? I asked myself. Prisoners had declared that there were two Reichstag buildings but they did not know which one was which.

Samsonov called Colonel Negoda. 'There is supposed to be another Reichstag. Which one should I take?' he asked.

The divisional commander pondered, then laughed: 'Take the one in front of you. Should it not be the right one, take the other one afterwards.'

Samsonov was lucky. His soldiers stormed the correct Reichstag.

CHAPTER FOUR

Few Know

After we had hoisted the flags on the Reichstag the fighting within the building continued for another two days and two nights. Hundreds of German soldiers that had been driven back from the Baltic to Berlin had entrenched themselves in the cellars of the Reichstag. They showered us with explosives using Panzerfausts. The Reichstag building went up in flames.

It burned like any other building: the fire found sufficient material – the furnishings burned, the wall coverings, the floors. Smoke and flames poured out of the windows. About 300 of our soldiers fought in the burning building.

On the morning of 1 May – the 1,410th day of the war – the Soviet Information Bureau made it known that our troops had taken the Reichstag and that the flag of victory had been hoisted.

In Paris, London and New York thanksgiving services were held. Bells ringing were heard on all radio stations.

But at this time our soldiers were standing on a floor in the burning Reichstag protecting their eyes from the suffocating smoke.

The battalion commander was ordered to withdraw his troops. 'Leave the Reichstag and adopt an all-round defence! Occupy the building as soon as it has burnt out!'

But the fire prevented their return. The soldiers put on gas masks. Suddenly a wall collapsed near them. Thick yellow smoke rolled up to the troops. Not a new danger, but rather an opportunity.

Our chaps climbed through the hole that had appeared unexpectedly in the adjoining room, which had already been burnt out. The fire destroyed the whole of the interior of the building, but not our flags. They fluttered undamaged on the Reichstag and were only slightly blackened.

Once the fire had been extinguished all the cellar entrances were blocked up again.

The morning of 2 March dawned.

V.K. Boitschenko told me about those who had fought on the far side of the Brandenburg Gate. A 'Hero of the Soviet Union' with whom

I had become acquainted in Jessentuki, Viktor Kusmitch Boitschenko was the commander of the reconnaissance platoon.

We fought for nearly a whole week on the Unter den Linden. It was hard to know who was fighting where. And the orientation was also difficult, it was worse than being in a wood. Everything was destroyed, if you took a street one had to find out what it was called.

We needed almost a week to take the Unter den Linden, this last metre. We had arrived between 23 and 25 April, and now we were firmly entrenched in this street. There was nothing to do; there was no possibility of going further. Nevertheless we went forward very slowly. There was crossfire from the right and the left. And the Brandenburg Gate was right in front of our eyes. The regimental commander summoned me to join him. He said that he had the following idea. My scouts should sit on the tanks and break through the gate.

I replied that we would not be able to do so in our current circumstances. Before we would have reached the Brandenburg Gate the tanks would have been shot up. We would have had to take it with the fire from guns and Panzerfausts. We would be fired on from the flanks from every window and building. Then it was proposed to have the tanks drive in three ranks, so that the middle ones could break through even if the tanks on the flanks went up in flames. In addition, in this situation obstacles could be expected. Apart from this it was not enough to reach the Brandenburg Gate. We had to go on to attack the Reichstag. As we could see, the gate was walled up and we did not know if there was a way through to the Reichstag.

But the commander told me that I should prepare the group. Then I told him I would take the leading tank and he would go in the second one.

We fought for another two days for every individual building, taking one after another and this way pushing halfway along the street. In the night leading to 1 May we discovered that elements of the 3rd Shock Army had taken the Reichstag and hoisted a flag. The resistance was weaker, and on 1 May we reached the Brandenburg Gate.

CHAPTER FIVE

On Königsplatz

'Calling, calling, calling', the telephonist said doggedly. She got no reply. The ten men that had gone to repair the line had not returned. One had fallen before reaching the site of the damage, the others on the way back.

But the telephone was working again. Neustroyev gripped the ear piece. Ilja Sjanov, who commanded an assault company, reported to the battalion commander: 'The enemy is assembling for an attack towards the Brandenburg Gate.' He asked for the street to be brought under fire.

Again there was a well-known whizzing sound over us and heavy shells ripped up the asphalt.

On this day – it was one of the most strenuous days of the war – there was bitter fighting on the square in front of the Reichstag. Our soldiers were lying near the Reichstag and were constantly attacking. The fire nests were still active. At all the windows, in the tanks and on the corners and in the self-propelled artillery in the depths of the parks.

A hardly identifiable red wire went across the square – the telephone line that connected the soldiers in front of the Reichstag with the command post and the observation post, directing the fire of the batteries. Splinters kept tearing the wire. But invisible hands patched it up and the connection kept on functioning.

Sjanov told me: 'There are tanks hidden right of the Reichstag.'

Our batteries opened fire and two tanks were destroyed.

As we occupied the building, the German soldiers had withdrawn to the cellars, and there was a pause in the fighting.

A soldier appeared at the battalion command post, which had already been moved to a small room in the Reichstag. His eyes were reddened and his blouse was torn. Vera Abramova, the battalion telephonist, considered him. She knew Alexey Melinkov. In the difficult hours he had repaired the line with the others. He went silently up to the telephone apparatus standing in the corner, crouched down and pulled on the crank. Melinkov had not come to talk about how he had

had to hide in the craters, how difficult it had been finding the breeches in the cable and how he had dealt with them. His eyes were red because he had not slept for many days.

The Commander put down the earphones and went across to him. 'Have your repaired the line?'

'Yes, sir!'

CHAPTER SIX

'Colonel' Berest

A white flag was suddenly hoisted from a cellar window. On the steps appeared an officer with an open greatcoat and a pistol in his hand. He announced that the German command was prepared to negotiate and wanted to speak to a high-ranking Soviet officer.

The choice fell on Berest. Berest was the battalion commander's political deputy and had been a lieutenant for a few days. The confirmation of his promotion had reached us as we entered Berlin. However he had been Neustroyev's deputy for some months already. Alexei Berest was 20 years old.

Berest put on a long leather jacket that did not belong to him. Captain Matveiev from the political department gave him his cap, which was new and crimson coloured.

Neustroyev accompanied him. He took off his padded jacket so that his medals could be seen. Berest did not have as many decorations to show.

A soldier that the Fascists had taken for forced labour went with them as interpreter. He had been liberated by us a few days earlier. He was 18, at most 20 years old, small, slender and had blonde hair.

The cellar where the Germans were waiting was lit by a torch. German soldiers holding pistols surrounded them, their helmets covered in camouflage netting. A German colonel, two younger officers and a female interpreter came up to Berest and his escort. The soldiers stood well apart.

The colonel reached for Berest's hand, but the latter put his right hand to his cap and said: 'Colonel Berest'.

He stood there in his black leather jacket, tall and young, the deputy of the commander, imposing, broad-shouldered and self-assured. One German said: 'So young and already a colonel!'

Neustroyev almost did not react at all, his shining medals looked stolen. He held himself decidedly back. Next to Berest the stocky Neustroyev looked even smaller: 'I suggest to you that you surrender!' said Berest to the Germans. 'Your situation is hopeless.'

The colonel replied: 'It is not yet certain who should yield to whom. You are 300 men. We are ten times more.'

'Surrender', demanded Berest. 'Or you will not get out of here.' And he looked at his watch to show that he wanted the talk to come to an end.

They tried to explain to Berest that our people were in a trap. Then the Fascist colonel unexpectedly demanded the chance to withdraw. Berest controlled himself only with difficulty. He was young, only 20 years old, and had forgotten that he was here to act as a diplomat. 'We have not come to Berlin to let you monsters go', he said. 'If you do not surrender, not one of you here will come out alive.'

The Fascist protested: 'Colonel! That is not the way one talks as a parliamentarian!'

Berest turned away. The young officers did not say a word. The female interpreter was nervous. Suddenly the German colonel began to speak Russian and did so tolerably well. 'We know our situation, and we want to surrender. But your soldiers are excited. Let them parade in front of the Reichstag so that they can see us!'

'No!' replied Berest. 'I have not come from Moscow to Berlin to have my soldiers paraded in front of yours. Even if you were 2,000 men and we 200.'

There was no point in continuing. Berest saluted, as did Neustroyev.

The interpreter and Neustroyev, who climbed the stairs behind Brest, heard how 'Colonel' Berest murmured ahead of them: '*Halunke! Halunke!*' – 'Scoundrel! Scoundrel!'

The Germans in the underground cellars of the Recihstag surrendered that same night.

CHAPTER SEVEN

We Will Not Forget the Dead

Among the names of the soldiers and officers that took the Reichstag the name Pyatnizki is unforgotten, Pyotr Pyatnizki. He was the one who, on the morning that the attack began, was the first to jump out of the window of the Ministry of the Interior. On the Spree the soldiers took cover. Suddenly a soldier rose up, unfolded a red flag and charged forwards. That was Pyotr Pyatnizki.

Our soldiers followed him. As they went up the steps to the entrance, the flag flared ahead of them. Then the man with the flag sank down. That was Pyatnizki.

His flag was hoisted on the Reichstag next to the other flags, but his had a special fate.

Towards evening, after the artillery preparation, a new attack took place, the soldiers of his battalion storming the Reichstag. Pyatnizki lay with the banner in his hands before the entrance. He was carried aside and laid down near a pillar.

And then they forgot him. When they remembered him, he had already been buried in a mass grave, apparently in the Tiergarten.

Pyotr Pyatnizki, a simple soldier, a fighter. A few days before the storming of the Reichstag he had been promoted to junior sergeant and became a runner for the battalion commander.

He is dead. His wife lives in a village in the Bryansk area, the widow Jevdokiya Pyatnizkaya and her now grown-up son. For many years they have regarded their father as missing. Pyatnizki come to our division shortly before the offensive on the Vistula. I cannot relate much about him. I would only report how on 30 April 1945 he ran over the square and he sank down with the flag before the doors of the Reichstag. He should remain unforgotten.

CHAPTER EIGHT

The Victory Flag

The flag of victory on the Reichstag dome was hoisted by Yegorov and Kantara. But there were other flags also raised on the Reichstag building. I will tell you about two brave men that did not come from Neustroyev's battalion like Kantara and Yegorov, but from Vassili Davydov's battalion. I will tell you of the flag that they carried and hoisted on the Reichstag.

There were only the two of them, the firing having cut them off from the rest. They knelt under the bridge under the cover of the not very high Spree embankment. It was not far to the Reichstag. They saw the massive pillars and the steps to the main entrance. But they could not come forward.

They were unable to raise their heads. The Germans were firing from the upper storeys of the Reichstag. Our soldiers lay under cover in the ditches and by lumps of dug-up asphalt.

Bulatov, a small man, lay close to Koshkarbayev. He was almost still a boy, the field blouse hanging like a sack on him, and his cap was also too big. 'What shall we do?' Bulatov asked his superior.

Koshkarbayev was the platoon commander, a lieutenant, and Bulatov was a soldier in his platoon. Koshkarbayev was from Kasakstan, Bulatov a Russian from Viatka.

And Koshkarbayev said: 'If it works, we will at least hoist our flag on the steps of the Reichstag.'

Koshkarbayev had wrapped the flag in black-out paper and stuffed it under his jacket. They called it a flag, although it was only a piece of thick red material. They decided to write their names on the cloth. With a dampened pencil they hastily wrote their names, and a somewhat deeper '674', the number of the regiment and their unit.

Our people attacked again towards evening. The first attack, led by Pjatnizki, was shattered, the group being wiped out. The attack by Sjanov's was joined by the soldiers of the two other battalions.

Koshkarbayev and Bulatov jumped up from their cover and charged towards the main entrance, where there was a screen and bricked-up windows. Bulatov and Koshkarbayev fastened their flag to the middle column. Once the left-hand side of the building had been cleared, they raised it to a window on the second floor.

It did not wave from the dome like that of Yegorov and Kantara, but out of a Reichstag window.

CHAPTER NINE

We Went Back on the Fifth Day

The enemy were close on our heels. We were hungry and barefoot, none of us had boots. We had to break through the ring that was getting ever tighter. There were only five or six of us. We carried our unit flag between us, sometimes one, sometimes another.

I recalled a day five years ago.

We had been standing in front of the school since early morning. On the road well-dressed people were marching festively in the May Day demonstration. We marched along the road to the village Soviet, and over us flew the Red Flag.

We were to break out during the night. We rolled the flag, our unit flag, around the body of a comrade and hid it under his field blouse and set off again. It was a dark night and we had a difficult time, but we came through.

A year passed. Snow lay around us, but there was a warm swamp that did not freeze and a narrow path leading over it. Behind the swamp rose a hillock cut through by a trench. A dark wood was visible on the horizon.

Every metre of the hillock was fired on. Nevertheless we got up, leaving our trenches and took the path through the swamp in single file to the other trench, which rose grey in the snow. And the Red Flag was still with us.

Another two years went past.

In the morning we saw behind the square not far from us the building that was our goal. A lieutenant, a soldier and yet another soldier were tearing at the red ticking of a featherbed.

When ran across the square that evening, the cloth hung over them like a flag. As morning broke we all saw the red cloth on a column, and high above on the dome the victory flag was waving.

CHAPTER TEN

The Victory Flag

The flag, known as the Victory Flag, is displayed in the Army Museum in Moscow. It was hoisted on the Reichstag building on 30 April 1945.

Before the attack on Berlin, the War Council of the 3rd Shock Army handed out red flags to all its divisions. There were nine of them, corresponding to the number of divisions in that Army. The flags were numbered. The flag handed over to the 150th Idriz Division bore the number 5.

On 26 April the divisional commander, General Shatilov, and the head of the political department, Artiuchov, gave the flag to the 756th Regiment, commanded by Colonel Sintshenko, which was to participate in the storming of the Reichstag.

The flag was placed in the regiment's observation post. Komsomol Fiodorov carried it. He was a brave soldier.

When the Interior Ministry building was occupied on 29 April, two battalions of the 150th Division and a battalion of the neighbouring 171st Division were in front of the Reichstag. Kantara and Yegorov were scouts of the regimental reconnaissance unit. At the Reichstag they fought in their regiment's 1st Battalion, Neustroyev's battalion. On 30 April Yegorov and Kantara went through the main entrance of the Reichstag with others. They dragged the flag through the building before reaching the dome. At 2250 hours they reported the flag hoisted on the Reichstag.

At that time the flag carried no inscription. In the upper corner next to the shaft only the hammer and sickle were shown. But when the flag was later taken on parade in Moscow it held an inscription – the divisional title.

Now one can read on the flag: 150 Idriz Division, Bearer of the Order of Kutusov IInd Class; 79th Rifle Corps, 3rd Shock Army, 1st Byelorussian Front.

I questioned them then for a long time, but hardly noted down anything apart from their names and short biographies. Yegorov and Kantara.

I discovered only that they had found themselves on the Spree bank 30m in front of the infantry, that Berest, the battalion commander's deputy, had been with them in the Reichstag when they were at the entrance looking for a way to go up, and that they had raised the flag a little later. Some details appeared to be lacking, but I will recount them for you.

Fighting was still going on inside the Reichstag above them and also below them. It was difficult to orientate themselves in the gloom, the windows having been bricked up. They did not know where the passages led to. And where should they raise the flag? Nobody had told them. Certainly as high as possible, so that it could be seen from far off.

They had thought that it was already dark. At last they found some stairs leading up to the roof. How far one could see! Shell splinters flew over them. It was good that the roof was flat. Where should they hoist the flag? There was a bronze horseman standing there. But no, he was not suitable. It looked as if he was holding the flag.

More splinters swept over the roof. They had to get a move on!

The best place was the dome.

The stairs swayed. They were badly damaged and were full of holes. Then they reached the frame of the dome. The iron ribs were far apart. All the glass had gone, but they took care not to look down, where the assembly room yawned. They hung as over an abyss. Their hearts were gripped by the cold.

From the dome they climbed up to the platform. They were dizzy, they weren't used this they weren't structural engineers. Just don't look down! Silently they fastened the flag with a strap.

Then they went back down again as quickly as they could.

In Siberia and in the Urals there is an old custom. In the middle of the village on the eastern side a smooth, tall mast is erected at Easter. Before it is erected the village maidens decorate it themselves by attaching nuts and sweets to it. They then find a young lad to climb to the top of the swaying pole to collect these gifts.

In a mine-workers' village in the Urals, near Sverdlovsk, year after year the same lad, son of a gold miner, got the prize. He was of medium size and his face was full of pock marks. Perhaps he had followed in his father's footsteps and also became a gold miner.

On 30 April 1945 he hoisted the flag on the Berlin Reichstag building.

CHAPTER ELEVEN

Schtscherbina

I have an old photograph of a group of soldiers standing on the steps of the Reichstag taken shortly after the battle. There are officers and soldiers. Their uniforms are torn and dirty and they have a scorched coat hung over their shoulders. Who are soldiers and who officers it is impossible to say.

One step lower than the others stands a soldier with a bandaged head. The bandage gleams white over the blackened brows. The young soldier standing one step lower down has puttees. He holds a machine-pistol in his hands. The sleeves of his blouse are rolled up. A true picture of war, I think. They are standing on the steps of the Reichstag, which is still burning. Who are these soldiers, and who is he?

I know little about him. I have only talked with him once, the day after the taking of the Reichstag. Previously I had never met him. He is Schtscherbina.

When I met him he had already been so pestered by the correspondents that he had hidden from them. And that was not surprising. After a week of incessant fighting he had still not slept. Nevertheless we sat on the advertising pillar opposite the main entrance.

Schtscherbina, Pyotr Dorofeyevitch, born in 1926 in the village of Skelka in Saporoshye Province. He got a head wound in Berlin, but could not be bothered to go to the dressing station. He described the experiences of the last days and the last fighting in this manner:

We jumped out of the windows of the Ministry of the Interior one after another, the first to jump being Pyatnizki. We crossed over the square, Rudnev, Novikov and Prochoshi running near me. The firing was particularly intense. We reached the steps and ran up them.

We occupied a big room. The cellars were full of Fascists. They threw hand grenades and fired Panzerfausts at us, dust falling from above. But we stood at the cellar entrances and fired back.

Then fire broke out somewhere. It was hot. The building filled with smoke. The fire soon reached us and we could no longer stay.

We climbed through an opening into another room. Then we came to a narrow passage and changed over to the non-burning part of the building.

We did not leave the Reichstag. Once the fire had been extinguished, we renewed our attack on the cellar.

In fact the situation was far more dramatic. Yes, Schtscherbina was with Pyatnizki. Their group was the first to reach the Reichstag entrance. When the rooms filled with smoke and the Fascists undertook a counterattack, our lads pulled back.

'Where are you going? Stay in your places!' called Schtscherbina.

Our soldiers took cover and fired at the Fascists as soon as they appeared. They went through corridors and rooms, the smoke biting their eyes, the soldiers becoming giddy.

A wall collapsed when it was hit by a shell. Fortunately no one was buried under the rubble.

Schtscherbina discovered a staircase leading upwards. 'Follow me!' he cried, struggling for air. The others followed him. He was convinced that he would find a way out somehow.

They went from room to room, through corridors and halls. Finally they reached part of the building in which the smoke had not yet penetrated and they could breathe freely.

As Kantara and Yegorov searched for the way to the roof to hoist their flag, Schtscherbina and some of his comrades gave them covering fire.

Junior Sergeant Pyotr Dorofeyevitsh Schtscherbina was decorated with the Order of the Red Banner on the square in front of the Reichstag.

Pyotr Schtscherbina and Pyotr Pyatnizki – two war veterans, two heroes – were good friends. Pyotr Pyatnizki was over 30 and head of a family, Schtscherbina was an unmarried lad with his mother waiting for him at home.

CHAPTER TWELVE

The Battalion Commander

Battalion Commander Neustroyev and I stood at the entrance for a while before crossing the square. He looked even smaller next to the Reichstag pillars. He looked tired.

After all the nights of staying awake he had still not slept it out of his system. He went along beside me. He wanted to show me where his battalion had fought.

The square was covered in stones, pieces of asphalt and splintered wood. From the bank of the Spree one could clearly see the damage to the Reichstag building. The blackened walls showed great holes. The columns looked like picket stakes that horses had nibbled.

I had known Neustroyev for a long time, and as I saw him standing on the broad steps of the Reichstag in front of the square over which the soldiers of his battalion had stormed, it brought to mind the small snow-covered village of Poplavy in the Kalinin area.

The fighting near Poplavy had begun in the autumn of 1943. But the Fascists had brought fresh forces and a lot of equipment into this sector so that our offensive came to a standstill. But after about two months, our artillery began to speak again in the winter. And as I went into the front-line trenches I heard from the other side of the white hillock a long drawn-out call – the infantry were attacking.

In a half-destroyed dugout – there were many there – I found the regimental commander in front of a radio set. He was reporting: 'The battalion has broken through the enemy defence. The battalion is commanded by Captain Neustroyev.'

I was unable to meet Captain Neustroyev that day. I heard his name again a month later, this time in the fighting for Staika village. Once more I had no opportunity of meeting him. The other division's battalion commanders I already knew and I had become friends with one of them.

Then the division received the order to construct a defensive position on the Velikaya River. The snow had vanished and the first shoots of grass were coming through the previous year's leaves. A small man in a tight uniform jacket, his boots thickly covered with red mud, was trudging along the foremost line. He stopped at one position and said something to the soldiers, whose heads were all that could be seen, and showed them where they had to dig. He went from soldier to soldier and inspected the new trenches, foxholes and machine-gun nests. That was Neustroyev.

We seldom saw each other. I realized later that he avoided encounters with newspaper people. During a break for a smoke – we were lying on a hillock alongside the Velikaya in the middle of a wood – he told me a little about himself. He came from the Urals, from the town of Beresovsk, near Sverdlovsk. 'A town standing on gold', he said. He had grown up in the Urals, where his parents and sister lived.

The division pushed on fighting. Many roads had to be crossed, many heights taken before we reached Lettland. Poland, Pomerania, the Oder.

Neustroyev was wounded five times. Once the dugout in which he was standing was hit by a shell. All were buried alive. Neustroyev, badly wounded, was able to get out.

All of all these things came to mind when I saw Neustroyev on the steps of the Reichstag.

CHAPTER THIRTEEN

How Wars End

Often we tried to foresee how it would be. War, war and suddenly peace. I once heard soldiers talking to a sergeant major in a dugout who had been in the Finnish war.

'So we took Vyborg', said the sergeant major. 'I was a runner and on my way with a message. In the wood I came across one of our soldiers.

"What do you want?" he asked me.

I stopped. "Why are you asking?"

"The war is over!" he said.

"You are lying!" I did not believe him. Angrily I shouted at him: "Why are you lying? Don't you know you could be shot?"

He replied: "Yes. But the firing will stop from twelve o'clock."

'At eleven forty-five,' so the sergeant major said, 'I was wounded. When I recovered consciousness, I was lying in the snow. An unusual quiet reigned around me. Then I understood that the war was over.'

I recalled this conversation several times when we thought about the end of the war.

This war will end differently, I said to myself. However I saw myself in my thoughts going over a field or through a wood, alone, as usual. A soldier came running up to me. Laughing and swinging his arms. I go past him, not knowing that the soldier knows something that I don't know yet.

That the sudden end of this war, although longed for, would be unexpected was obvious to all of us. Someone had said to us at the beginning of the war that it would last four years, but we had not believed him.

We had already driven the enemy out of our country and the war was still going on. We took Berlin. The fighting died down. Another week went past. One morning Mitya woke me with the words: 'Lieutenant, get up! The war is over!'

Wars end in various ways – this war ended his way.

CHAPTER FOURTEEN

White Mammoths

The bare trees were covered with frost. The frost-hard snow crunched under our feet.

The town lay in the region of eternal winters, thousands and thousands of miles away from the war. Mysterious rumours circulated that the tanks built here rolled straight out of the factory into battle.

The light had just become grey in the windows when people in padded jackets filled the street. They had their heads drawn in, their faces hidden behind the highly drawn collars. All went in one direction, their breath hanging in the air like a cloud of steam. They went closely pressed together in two dark rows in the grey dawn. The snow fallen in the night was black under their feet.

Smoke rose from the factory chimneys.

On the fence near the pavement a placard hung over the people's heads: 'To arms comrades!'

The people on the pavement finally came up against the rows of workers that had completed their night shift.

Tanks rolled out of the factory gate, plump-looking monsters. The camouflage paintwork shone white despite the twilight. We called them white mammoths. As they rolled forward, our barracks alongside the road shook and quivered.

Worker after worker hurried into the factory.

Soviet guns cover troops charging towards the Reichstag from the Ministry of the Interior with the lip of the excavation for the Spree bypass behind them. The building beyond the tanks is the Swiss embassy, which is still there.

A Soviet machine-gun team in action.

Two Soviet tanks destroyed at the end of the Moltkestrasse with the flooded cutting for the proposed new course of the Spree beyond.

Soviet tanks negotiating a Berlin street.

After the battle debris in a Berlin street.

Soviet tanks near the Brandenberg Gate.

The Soviet flag over the Reichstag.

An aerial view of the Reichstag after the battle. Note the miscellaneous buildings used to prepare the construction site for Hitler's projected new city centre with 'The Great Hall of the People' and palaces for Hitler and Göring.

Inside the ruined
Reichstag.

Soviet soldiers'
inscriptions inside the
captured Reichstag.

Marshal Zhukov (centre) inspects the ruined Reichstag.

Soviet tanks outside the Reichstag.

An artist's impression of the Reichstag victory.

Celebrating the taking of the Reichstag.

Victorious besiegers
pose before their prize.

Soviet soldiers
inspecting discarded
German medal cases.

The Brandenberg Gate and Unter den Linden after the battle.

Defeat.

A Soviet soldier views the Reichstag.

CHAPTER FIFTEEN

Strike Your Weapons

In spring – it was in April – many years after the war we met in Moscow. Some of us bore the title of 'Hero of the Soviet Union'. We had grown older and everyone had changed in his own way.

General Vassili Mitrofanovitch Shatilov, our divisional commander, had gone grey. The youngest among us, Yegorov, was now a factory foreman and wore a blue peaked cap. He was ill, looked thin and had a box of bicarbonate of soda pills in his pocket. Sintshenko, regimental commander, now a reservist, was happy, cheerful and dressed in full parade uniform. Neustroyev had also come – erect as though he had become younger, once more an officer and wearing the shoulder badges of a lieutenant colonel.

These were turbulent days. Everyone was arriving in Moscow at different times and everyone was taken away to the homes of those they had already met. It went on like this for a whole week.

We visited the Army Museum, and the lively museum guide recounted how the Reichstag had been taken. With a pointer she indicated here and there. Sometimes she mixed up the names, but the comrades were happy and only laughed.

They toured Moscow and an expensive film was made of them. Davydov, with his usual good-natured but sick-looking face, had to go with his shotgun on his back to hunt in the Siberian Taiga. That was filmed at the Peredel Cinema, where snow was still on the ground.

At the flag in the museum an encounter occurred with four young soldiers, who had been adrift in the ocean for forty-nine days. They had been brought back to their country and Moscow had already given them a reception. When they saw the original version of the film they in the main were surprised by the old pictures. Saluting on the roof of the Reichstag. They had been children then – exactly fifteen years had passed.

Our comrades lived in a hotel, but almost every evening came to my place. In our apartment on the thirteenth storey my daughter experienced a bit of history. She looked at the men whose names she had learned in history lessons with wonder.

Syanov came to me once more before flying to Alma-Ata. He was deputy chairman of the local consumers association. We sat together for a long time and he stayed the night with us.

Soldiers like Ilya Syanov – towards the end of the war we encountered each other infreqently – had been there since the 'founding of the division' we always said. He was born in Kustanai, where our 150th Division was raised. He was already no longer young then. In the thirties he had studied at the Workers' Academy and at the Party School. Before the beginning of the war Ilya Jakovlevitch Syanov had worked as a bookkeeper.

On the day that the Reichstag was stormed Senior Sergeant Syanov took over command of a company. That occurred in the morning at the Ministry of the Interior. He came straight to his battalion as the soldiers were being fired upon from the upper storeys, and no one dared raise their heads on the square in front of the Reichstag.

Syanov told me how his company had broken through the shattered door in the Reichstag on 30 April. It had had to fight in the unfamiliar, strongly barricaded building for one-and-a-half days. It was interesting to hear how various people speak of one and the same day.

I had laid myself down on the sofa. Our sofa is short and Ilya is long, so we had set up the camp-bed for him. Through the half-open air vent came the roar of the not – yet – quiet Moscow.

I had a habit of leaving the most important questions to the end. And when it seemed to me that we had exhausted all the important themes, I asked him to tell me how he had dealt with the Germans.

At the time I had only noted down one sentence as a record of this matter: 'Their handling was conducted by Sergeant Syanov'. Only this one sentence. Apart from this, I found no detail, no word about it in my notebook, in which so many heroics, so many courageous actions were recorded. That was not surprising, as my short notes could only serve as reminders. That was certainly the case.

However, it was surprising that I had not discussed things longer with Syanov as the column of prisoners of war was led away. He told me about the soldiers in his unit who had distinguished themselves during the last of the fighting. But there is nothing in my notebook about his negotiations, nothing about himself.

In the confusion at that time I had forgotten to ask him how it was that he alone went into the S-Bahn tunnel to confer with a group of Germans.

Now, after so many years, Syanov recounted:

My company command post was in the dome and consisted of boxes. On my right were the stairs to the cellar. We could see them clearly.

In was during the night of the 1st to 2nd May. We had occupied the Reichstag up to the third floor. There were still fires in the building. The Fascists had barricaded themselves in the cellars.

At about two o'clock Neustroyev ordered me to hand over my sector to Second-Lieutenants Antonov and Gribov and give myself a break. Antonov was young, and had undergone his baptism of fire in the fighting in Germany.

I briefed both of them on the situation. I went off to eat at about three o'clock. Although the square was still under fire, we were well provided for.

Then Sergeant Major Malzev reported that my company had fallen in. Before the storming of the Reichstag we had amounted to eighty-three men, now there were only twenty-six. There had been times when we were unable to get the wounded out of the firing. We had more dead than wounded. I established that Jakomovitsh, Gusev, Itshanov and many other soldiers that had been allocated to my company as reinforcements were missing. I had not yet got to know all of them, and now they had already fallen.

The soldiers looked awful with burns and other wounds. Their coats were torn, their shoes burnt through, and from their boots jutted the rags and tatters of their footcloths. They looked silently at me, but I could see from their faces that they inwardly had not given up fighting. Now, however, they could rest. Fresh units had occupied our position.

I led my soldiers out of the building. We laid ourselves down right at the entrance, behind pillars and pressed close to the wall. The fresh air did us good. We immediately fell asleep.

I woke up when someone shook me by the shoulder, and immediately jumped up. Before I could call out the customary: 'Company to battle!' the messenger held my mouth and said that I was wanted in the observation post.

This was at about four o'clock. I had slept for an hour. There was still firing on the square, but not the Reichstag when I entered it.

About twenty officers were standing in a small room on the left-hand side. I saw some new faces among them. Gussev and Prelov were also there. Prelov smiled at me.

'What's happening?' I asked.

Gussev, our chief of staff, replied: 'We want to dress you up well.' And the Battalion commander's batman handed me a new greatcoat and boots.

I did not understand. A major joked that no one intended marrying me, it was an order. And he explained: 'The German Command has requested negotiators by radio to deal with the capitulation of the German troops in Berlin. We want to send you as a negotiator in the rank of a general. We do not regard this as valid for long. Make sure that you are ready at the agreed time.

Gussev said: 'An interpreter [his name was Dushinski, Viktor Borislavovitsh], a staff-sergeant, and a runner will accompany you. The fighting will cease from four to six o'clock when the negotiations will take place. The whole thing will be up to you. The escort will carry a white flag [it was already prepared], and they will light your way.'

He gave me a large pocket torch. On our way the interpreter would call out in Russian and in German: 'Soviet and German soldiers – don't shoot – we are parliamentarians.'

'What conditions should I set?' I asked.

'Unconditional surrender ... Unconditional surrender on the basis of the decisions made at the Yalta Conference. Say that the officers can keep their side arms.'

I then asked how the capitulation should proceed.

'Tomorrow they form up and come out with illuminated white flags,' he replied.

I washed myself before putting on the new boots and greatcoat. The pocket torch I hung from my chest. We shook hands and went outside, turning left for the Brandenburg Gate.

We were informed by radio that the German parliamentarians would meet us at the S-Bahn station entrance. On my left went the runner with the flag, on my right the interpreter.

I had just illuminated the white flag, which the soldier was carrying high, when there was the rattle of machine-gun fire. We threw ourselves down and crawled forward a bit. We were confused.

There was no cover anywhere. We debated and decided to go round the building on the northern side, where there was a well-fortified German trench now occupied by our infantry.

We managed the advance and reached the trench. Standing in front of the entrance to the S-Bahn we saw a group of about fifteen men. We were still some distance away when someone called out to us in Russian telling us not to go any further. We stayed still. Several officers came closer. I called out: 'Lower your weapons!' One officer had a pistol in his hands. He immediately put it away, but demanded that we left our weapons at the entrance. 'Parliamentarians must be unarmed.'

A burnt-out tank stood nearby. We laid our machine-pistols, hand grenades and my pistol on its tracks. We fastened our holsters. The Germans waited. Then they came up to us and the oldest officer said: 'Follow us!'

We climbed down inside. Three went in front, the remainder behind us, the officers going ahead of us repeatedly saying: 'Make way. Make way.' There were no uniformed people here, only civilians. We noticed many wounded. Two well-dressed men pressed through to us and said: 'We are Russians.'

I did not believe them, they did not look right.

The way seemed endless to us. And quite honestly, we were not happy. I was afraid that we had been caught in a trap. Incensed faces looked at us. Two generals joined us, each with an interpreter as escort. A weak light sparingly lit the tunnel. We went on and on and I asked myself if I would ever see daylight again. Then we reached a station that gave me the impression we were in a large room, and stood there.

The German officers wanted to know our conditions and whether we would shoot them or we would guarantee them safe conduct.

One asked the name of our commander. To impress them I named as many as possible, Marshals Rokossovski, Konev, Zhukov, Generals Bersarin, Shatolov. I also promoted Negoda to the rank of general, and named Sintschenko and Perevertkin, adding that Kusnezov's army was also here.

The generals retreated a little and vanished behind a door, apparently into a room for station personnel. Two sentries stood in front of it.

We were surrounded by officers and soldiers. My apprehension grew. We had already waited 10 minutes. Where were the generals? My escorts were also worried.

Finally the generals returned. The door behind them remained open. One of them said something. The interpreter translated: 'Our command is not here. We don't know where it is.'

My runner came up to me wanting to say something: 'They have led us astray!'

Later I discovered that the commander in chief of the Berlin defence, General Weidling, without waiting for our command's representatives, had gone to Chuikov's headquarters to arrange the capitulation.

I asked: 'What is this? You asked us for parliamentarians and now there is no one to deal with here? Is this a game?'

We were assured that really there was no one there with the authority to negotiate.

'Good', I said, 'We don't know where your headquarters are. But you yourselves are commanders and can decide for your troops. I demand that you surrender and leave the tunnel.'

I reminded myself that, some days before, Berest, himself as a parliamentarian, had gone into the cellars of the Reichstag and returned without success. The Fascists were hoping to gain time this way. They had been told that a new formation was on the march to Berlin, the Wenk Army.

I explained to them that they were apparently awaiting the arrival of this army, which had long since been eliminated. My words seemed to have some effect on them. I then decided to end the talks. I demanded an escort to accompany us to the entrance.

'Two men will escort you', a general declared.

We set off on the way back. I kept looking at my watch as I feared we had gone over the time limit. The hand was getting closer to six. We had to hurry up and went faster. I heard the officers following us striding out. The return route seemed twice as long. It was just a few minutes to six o'clock.

Suddenly someone called out: 'Stop! Stand still!' Soldiers blocked the way.

We stood still and were certain that we would get a shot in the neck. Several officers and the two generals came up to us. They hastily explained to us that they wanted to surrender with their soldiers.

Shouts and orders erupted. There was a shot, but only one.
The Germans threw down their weapons.

It was already gone six o'clock when we climbed the steps to the street, officers and soldiers following us. We made our way to the Reichstag building with a group of officers.

Gussev and a major, who had been wounded by a splinter in his head during our absence, were waiting for us anxiously. They had had the same fear, that the Fascists could have lured us into a trap.

Weidling later signed the surrender document.

CHAPTER SIXTEEN

My City Guide

Berlin had capitulated, but the war was not yet over. I decided to have a look around the city, and it was the centre that I did not know. I left the Reichstag building and went across the square to the Brandenburg Gate.

It was dark and cool under the archway. The wide passages between the columns were blocked with bricks. Only the narrow passages at the sides were passable. Somehow the gate was crooked. This could be because many shells had hit the masonry and torn out pieces of the stonework.

It began to rain, although the sky above me was still blue. May rain! Big drops splashed on the ground. There was no better place to look for shelter than under the gate. No drops got through there.

I stood and looked at the framework of the burnt-out, smoke-blackened, destroyed buildings over which the rain was pouring and the wet, torn asphalt and noticed a soldier leaning against a pillar with a dangling rifle. He had apparently got here before me. He was no longer young. A moustache adorned his face and on his head the soldier wore a reddish, crushed cap with ear muffs. Ear muffs had not been worn for some time. Berlin had been conquered in caps.

I spoke to him and wrote in my notebook, just like a brand new journalist, 'Soldier Andryiushin'. The soldier was not concerned with what I wrote. For him it was the most normal thing in the world, or nearly so.

After a few general sentences I realized that the Brandenburg Gate, under which we were standing, covered the whole width of the street. The soldier nodded and declared that that he had been in Berlin once before. I took it that he was one of the soldiers that had joined up with us after having been a prisoner. But he denied this.

'So, in the First World War?' I asked him.

The soldier shook his head. 'No! Before the First World War! I visited Berlin in 1912 with the pupils of the St Petersburg Imperial Lyceum.' No, he had not been a pupil himself, and he had not given lessons at the Lyceum either. He had worked there as a porter. And they had also driven through this gate. He drew my attention to the massive construction. He knew it but somehow it seemed strange to him.

Meanwhile other soldiers had sought shelter from the rain under the Brandenburg Gate. They were soaked through. All were unarmed, wearing puttees and faded caps. They were holding bunches of lilacs – blooming lilacs.

Many lilacs grow in Berlin, in overgrown areas, near ruins, and they seemed especially luxuriant this spring. Their scent was so strong that it smothered all other smells, even that of the corpses, and lasted longer.

Lilacs in the city, unbelievably beautiful lilacs, a uniquely beautiful spring!

Soldiers, men that had stood up to firing, were going through the city holding lilacs in their hands. And the scent of the lilacs excited us. It seemed so unreal and yet so meaningful, because the smell of gunpowder and fires had not yet vanished from the streets. We seemed to be drunk.

It had stopped raining. The soldiers with the branches of lilac in their hands had moved on. The sun broke through the clouds.

Kirill Jegorovitch led me along the straight, wide street of Unter den Linden, with the water steaming on the asphalt. I was going along this street for the very first time. This is where the Fascists had continued their resistance after we had already taken the Reichstag. I was delighted to have met a soldier who had already been to Berlin once before. Although everything looked different, much was destroyed, but my companion had a good sense of orientation and an even better memory. On my own it would have very difficult to find my way. It was different during the fighting, when the regiment or battalion was assigned a specific sector and one thrust forward from one designated point to another. That was how we had thrust forward from the north-western districts of Berlin to the Reichstag. Now the fighting was over. I could go where I wanted without hindrance. Then I realized that it was not quite so easy. I had no military map, no city plan. I neither knew the main streets nor which district I was in or what it was called.

This is why I felt safe alongside Kirill Jegorovitch. He had been here before, he knew the place.

Sculptures stood on the ledges of the destroyed and burnt-out buildings. Undamaged, the bronze was adorned with green patina and the statues looked as if made of opaque glass.

My companion became animated when he saw a building richly adorned with reliefs and ornaments. We looked inside through window grilles. There were so many weapons! Cannon, mortars and muskets apparently stemming from past days and centuries. We were standing in front of the Zeughaus, the museum of military history.

And more yawning windows, fallen walls, patina-decorated bronze, fields of rubble and ruins, ruins and fields of rubble. Everything had looked quite different, said Kirill Jegorovitch.

I knew the Unter den Linden from picture postcards. This wide parade street through which once had marched the imperial and later the Fascist soldiers. How many of them now lay under Soviet earth? And yesterday long irregular columns of prisoners had been escorted along this street.

We crossed the Spree Bridge – it was the only one not destroyed – and went along to the Lustgarten. We stood in front of the cathedral, and in front of the palace, both bearing the scars of war. Soldiers lay sunbathing or sleeping in the sun at the foot of a cavalry memorial. Sleep was now the most important thing.

I told Kirill Jegorovitch that several days ago I had looked at the Victory Column in the Tiergarten between toppled trees and burnt-out tanks.

Kirill Jegorovitch grinned through his yellowish, smoky beard and said the soldiers had christened the gilded statue as 'The women's toilet with wings'.

Today I can no longer recall why I had not attempted to see the Reichs Chancellery. Perhaps I thought that one could not go in. Perhaps it was also because I did not have confidence in Kirill Jegorovitch. Naturally he did not know the New Reichs Chancellery that Hitler had had built and so could not take me in.

Kirill Jegorovitch, who at the start had been such a good visitor's guide, gradually became quiet on the way. Many years had passed since his visit to Berlin and much had changed.

So it happened that not he but I took the lead. I went with him along random streets, driven on by my curiosity.

Finally we turned back. We got back to the Unter den Linden and went along the other side of it this time. The Brandenburg Gate was right in front of us as we went along a neighbouring street that was not very wide and moreover did not appear to have any attractions. One street sign still remained, and I read 'Wilhelmstrasse'.

I considered what context I had heard this name before. Then I remembered. I turned left, much to the bewilderment of Kirill Jegorovitch, who did not understand why we were not going to the Reichstag.

We stood in Hitler's study. Part of the ceiling had fallen in and the sun shone through the hole. The floor was covered in broken furniture, paper, stones and a lot of dust. The room was very big, like a hall. Books lay in the bookcases, many bound in black. The desk took up a lot of room.

A door opened on to a park. The trees were – like so many trees in Berlin – blown apart, upturned, splintered. Two civilians, presumably foreign journalists, were going around looking among the trees.

Someone showed us the entrance to the bunker, where Hitler had been quartered during our storm on Berlin. After he had poisoned himself his body had been taken up to the garden to be burnt. Here he had been laid down on these cement panels covered with the ashes of the burned archives like a scorpion that had bitten itself.

As we were leaving the rubble we saw a large group of people on the street. A horse had collapsed and the hungry Berlins were falling on the meat.

Then we were back on the Unter den Linden and my old friend, the former porter from the Imperial Lyceum, was livelier. Gradually he resumed his original role and explained this and that to me. It was as if he was not showing me Berlin but the Lyceum, so assured he felt that here was the rector's room and there on the right was the Aula.

Many thanks, old chap, you have shown me a lot today.

The sun sank behind the dead buildings as we came to the Reichstag. Our sentry was standing outside the main entrance, talking loudly with two German civilians.

I took my leave of Kirill Jegorovitch, my city guide, took my leave of the Soviet soldier Kirill Jegorovitch.

CHAPTER SEVENTEEN

Encounter

It had become quieter and we found our way around eventually up the unending stairs and through the passages. It was light in the big conference room that was capped by the dome. The dome was holed and one could see the sky. There were stones and bricks lying on the floor, a confused mess.

Through a dark corridor, which was packed full of knightly armour, one came to a part of the building that had not been damaged by fire. Here too the walls were full of holes and it smelled of burning. An old submachine-gunner was sitting in a sumptuous leather chair. He was dirty and unshaven, not having had time to clean himself up. But the submachine-gun leaning on his chair was clean. He had a thick *papirosa* cigarette between his teeth.

He stretched out in his chair and I asked: 'How are you?'

'Fine. I'm sitting in the Reichstag.'

He looked at me smiling. He knew what it meant, that he was sitting in the Reichstag and he could imagine how he looked in this chair with his torn cap and faded uniform.

'I am sitting here.'

His smile seemed unfamiliar to me, and then I recognized him. He was the company clerk Garkusha, an old acquaintance of mine. A year-and-a-half ago, in the winter of 1943/44 – in the Kalinin area – he had participated in an attack on a Fascist position. Yes there were clerks like this! He too had recognized me. And now he was sitting in the Reichstag, Grigori Garkusha.

I went out into the square. It was warm, sunny and clear. There were some tattered trees near the entrance.

CHAPTER EIGHTEEN

Notes

We ended the war a whole week before the soldiers on other fronts. They still had the march on Prague ahead of them and had to close up to the Elbe.

No more shots fell in Berlin on the morning of 2 May. Smoke still rose from the rubble and the spring wind played with the cold ashes. It was a new feeling living without war!

It was a new feeling for me, for I was still young then. In my note-book were records of conversations with soldiers, reports on the fighting, brief notes on who had fought where. Until now I had been writing about war events, and suddenly I was making notes about the feelings we were experiencing now that the war appeared to have ended, for us at least.

For the first time in my role as a journalist I lived and wrote without thinking about the newspaper. I even wondered about writing something that the newspaper did not specifically need. I was writing for myself.

These notes came to me like small accounts forming a big picture. They contain much that could stimulate the reader's imagination, notes that I made on the battlefield on the day after the fighting. I had written them down between 2 and 9 May.

One can believe that the war is ended because there are so many prisoners everywhere. They are surrendering their weapons and there are piles of them on the street.

The Germans that had sat in the cellars and the upper storeys of the Reichstag had not only capitulated, but more than that, the whole of the Berlin group had given themselves up. One spoke of parachutists being left behind in the hinterland, but is that so? And if so, where is that hinterland?

At the Reichstag building stands the vast, colourful, thrown-together column of prisoners, half of whom are Volkssturm. German soldiers and officers pass through the Brandenburg Gate under our guard. What a picture!

The soldiers who died during the last minutes are being buried in the buildings where the surrounding foliage has been destroyed by debris. Their comrades stand there with their heads bowed. What agony in their pressed together lips. All their faces are as if made of stone.

'Eternal fame to those who gave their lives so that the flag of victory could be hoisted over Berlin.' This has been burnt with a ret-hot nail in the board. Everyone thinks of the comrades that did not survive this day. Many had fallen in the streets of Berlin.

The battalion command post has been established in a narrow room in the Reichstag building. This is where the mail is being sorted. Today many of us receive letters from home, from our distant homeland.

Michail Saizev has received some post. Now he has read the letter from his mother from Siberia, from the Agara, he is writing a reply:

Dear Mother, our unit has hoisted the flag on the Reichstag in Berlin. Perhaps you do not know what the Reichstag is, Mama. There are ruins after ruins in Berlin. I see Germans reeling from hunger. That has suddenly caught up with them. The war, Mother, is over. I have seen a lot and learned a lot. I have participated in some hard fighting. But all that is over. I will soon be coming back home, and we will live in style. Until then, goodbye Mother. Your son, Michail Saizev.

Our flags are waving everywhere, even on the Brandenburg Gate. Now the fighting is over, we go through Berlin, and although Berlin has surrendered and the fires have been extinguished, we distrust the silence.

On the Reichstag there is a sign with the word 'De-Mined'. These signs have appeared, 'The road to Berlin is De-Mined', since Warsaw. And now, finally, also on the Reichstag. 'De-Mined'. It is written in black paint and forces us to stop. It works like a full stop.

In the morning I climb out of the Reichstag cellar, where our unit's accommodation is, and look at many soldiers unknown to me. They are examining the building and chatting with participants in the fighting.

I go to the other side towards the Spree. There are many people here too. On the roadway stands a strong, stocky man with his legs wide apart. The man is looking around curiously. The pockets of his shabby naval jacket are stuffed full. Several pens shine in his breast pocket. He has a small camera clasped under one arm and a notebook under the other.

His elbows are firmly clasped so that he drops nothing. He is speaking with a soldier and writing eagerly in a book that he is holding in his hand. Vishnevski! That is how I saw him the first time.

Last year's leaves under our feet are slippery. Between the trees in the Tiergarten lie weapons that have already become rusty.

I go along a street in the park in which stand many memorials. Mohnke, Schlieffen, Bismarck. The Iron Chancellor is wearing a long frock coat and a peaked cap on his head. In front of him on the pedestal are lyres, stone book pages and a Cupid with a quiver full of arrows.

Behind the chancellor I see Siegfried, naked, strong, forging a sword. As I turn to leave I hear a second lieutenant announcing to his platoon: 'And they silently prepared for war.'

The German capitulation was talked about all day long. Every conversation turns to this, and when one meets someone the first question is: 'Is there anything new?'

One report after another comes from the radio. The last German towns have been occupied. We receive the news that in one day our people have taken prisoner half a million soldiers and officers.

A report is being circulated. The capitulation? We had not yet heard of it. Italian, Bulgarian, French words sound on the loudspeakers, all languages except German. The dial turns again and a choir sings.

That is England. Somebody is talking: the Prime Minister. So they can hurry when they want to! If it is necessary to stop church services and ring the bells, they do not delay. But they should have acted more quickly and not put off the Second Front for so long.

We get no rest that night. Fast footsteps, knocking at the doors, clattering on the steps. We run across the street, stumbling in the darkness. A faltering voice: 'It has already been reported on the radio ...'.

'Perhaps it is an error?'

'No, I heard it myself ...'.

The soldiers press in front of the loudspeaker, and although the room is dead silent, someone shouts: 'Quiet!'

I believe that I can hear my neighbour's heartbeat.

'To honour the victorious ending of the Great Fatherland War ... 9th May ... Victory Celebration Day.'

An elderly soldier lies down slowly on a stool. At the window stands Natashka Kononova, a girl from the field post office. She has buried her head so that no one can see her face.

Lieutenant Colonel Artyuchov reads the declaration of the capitulation of Germany. He is annoyed and keeps clearing his throat. 'I am extremely happy to bring you this news', he calls out. 'Allow me to congratulate you ...'.

'On this day of celebration we will not forget those that can no longer hear the word "peace"', said a large, gaunt soldier. I heard these stumbling, unrehearsed speeches and recalled another spontaneous meeting that had taken place on 22 July 1941 in the wood on the border where we faced the Fascist attack on our homeland.

A parade took place after today's meeting. The regimental flag was carried by Gavriil Chandogin, a well-known sniper and Siberian hunter.

Somebody was tossed in the air. The commanders were thrown up in the air, the soldiers sending them up one after another.

Many were wearing medals. One soldier who had only just come to the front from the reserves had no medals, but how he smiled!

Wherever one looked one saw happy, smiling eyes on this sunny, warmer day. The Germans watched us furtively. 'When the war ends ...'.

The older soldiers still cannot take it in that the war is over. We hear the news from the Soviet information offices.

I am sitting with Varenikov, thinking of our families and homes. Varenikov has a great longing: 'Bring me two glasses of water, our water and the water from here. I will distinguish between them and drink ours.'

We have often dreamed of sitting quietly at a table like this. We are talking about the Fascists. 'They saw Moscow through their binoculars and now we are in Berlin.'

Suddenly a gun fired outside. We rushed into the street. Flares were going up, the flak fired and guns thundered. This was the salute, the salute to the victory over Berlin.

We stood on the streets and could not see enough of the flares going across the sky. No shots, no explosions, unusual but good. How everything has changed so suddenly! One can think of the future and make plans which a few days ago would have been impossible.

How everything had changed so quickly! One could think of the future and make plans. Only a few days ago we had been unable to do this. We were looking at the world with different eyes. We were now seeing things that we had not seen the day before.

We looked at the trees and felt the rough bark. We breathed in the air deeply that was as clean as after a storm. How lovely it is. I want to touch the soft grass with hands and eyes, or take off my boots to feel the earth.

No shots, no explosions. Unusual, but good.

CHAPTER NINETEEN

The Base Camp

I am walking with the aid of a stick, having had a fall. I have been lying down for several days and become accustomed to its support. As it is difficult without it, my wife had bought the stick. She chose this one, although the woman selling it advised against it. It is short and looks like an axe with its grip. However it is a good stick, stable and light.

I go here and there tapping the rusty Moscow pavements. Despite the stick I have slipped dangerously in some places, and even fallen once. I am not completely unstable on my feet, certainly not. As far as I can remember this is only the second time in my life that I have needed support.

The war was already long over when I apparently lay in a German hospital for a long time. I used a stick for the first time when I got up and was able to walk through the streets again. It was the only personal item that I had taken with me to hospital and had not given it any particular thought. It was a normal mountain stick with small embellishments nailed to it. But it had a history.

After Berlin had capitulated we remained in the city for several weeks. One night we received the order to leave Berlin. In the army everything happened suddenly and with great alarm. We did not understand then why this haste was necessary. Then we discovered that the district of Berlin in which we were quartered was to become the British Sector.

It was deep in the night. We loaded our printing equipment in the vehicle, stowed away our rucksacks and overcoats and climbed in ourselves. The loading area of our one-and-a-half-tonner was like a tall box. Once the driver Mitya had raised the tailboard and fastened it, we crouched in deep darkness. So we sat in our hen coop next to one another until the column stopped and Mitya let us out.

But hardly had we stretched our aching backs then the order came to drive on, and we climbed back into our box.

We crossed Gross-Schonebeck and drove through a wood that reminded me of my homeland. Then I was disconcerted by the high wire fences on both sides of the road. It was not yet clear to me where we were when we stopped. Our vehicle stood not far from a villa. Someone threw our stuff out of the truck and we carried it into the house. We did not know what kind of house it was, but there was no one there we could ask.

I had been allocated a room on the first floor. I carried up my suitcase fully packed with notebooks and some copies of our divisional newspaper, and looked around. The room had a wide double window. The room was not big, and the floor was covered with photographs and illustrated magazines. I called Mitya, pointed to the floor and asked him to help clear away the papers.

Mitya, who had had no time to eat, gnawed at a piece of bread, nodded and vanished. That meant that he would fulfil my request as soon as he was able.

A massive wardrobe stood near the door. When I wanted to hang my overcoat and uniform jacket in it, I found that all kinds of things were already hanging inside, uniforms without shoulder tabs, hunting clothes, separate trousers and jackets. I took these items out and stuffed them in the laundry basket. It occurred to me that the things were very big. Four people of my build could have fitted into one of these jackets. There was a walking stick in one corner of the wardrobe, a strong walking stick.

I did not stay long in the room. I wanted to get outside to breathe some air and look around, so I took the stick with me.

There was nobody on the steps or in the truck. It looked like everyone had gone off separately. The building was so big that everyone had a room of his own. In recent days we had become used to living quietly. That was different to the past when we came through burnt-out places in the Soviet Union and Poland. There we had had laid down together in whatever room, happy to have a roof over our heads. Here even our printer had its own room.

I stood in front of the house for a while before going into the wood. The birches, spruces and pines all smelled. It was unusually quiet. I was aware of this silence for the first time since the war. It was not just the silence of the woods that impressed me, as it had in my childhood. It was another silence.

We had fought in woods. Near Kalinin we had erected ramparts of tree trunks, behind which we sought shelter because the trenches that we dug immediately filled with water. In Latvia, in Poland and also in Germany we had gone on fighting through the woods. Only a few months previously we had laid down in an apparently endless pinewood on the Oder. The wood was thus not unknown to me. Unfamiliar was the silence, this quite particular silence. The war had ended, the weapons were silent.

And this walk through the woods was my first encounter with nature since the war. Consequently I took note of it all, examining everything particularly remarkable – the rough trunks of trees, the drops of resin lighting up in the sunshine. Young greenery was breaking through the dead leaves. I stood with my back to the sun on a little hill, prodding the earth with my stick and turned over the rotting leaves. Then I looked at the stick. From handle to tip it was covered with postage-stamp-sized badges in tin. I counted sixteen. A castle could be seen on the first one, on the second a stately house. It must have belonged to a rich man, I thought.

An elderly man came towards me on my way. He held himself upright, although he seemed to have had a bad accident. I took him for a forester. He looked at me furtively and said something that I did not understand. I showed him the stick, pointed to the shields and asked him what significance it had for him. The old man felt along the stick with his hand, lingering over the middle badge, kept his finger on it and pointed with the other hand to the house in which I was quartered. I now recognized the picture on the shield. The old man pointed to the stick and said: 'Chief, nothing else'.

I did not understand what he meant. Then he tried to explain to me. Finally I understood that this stick had belonged to Hermann Göring.

I went back to the house and my room.

Mitya had not yet cleared the paper. I lifted up an illustrated magazine and leafed through it, and took the next one. There were pictures of Göring in both of them. I found no amateur photos. Göring with generals, Göring with his family, and one picture showing him with a group of soldiers in front of the house in which we now found ourselves. On the back I read: 'March, 1936'.

Why had they assembled here in this quiet woodland reserve? What secret plans had they been discussing? The picture offered no clues. I recognized one officer in the picture: Keitel.

When he was about to be hanged, Göring had taken his life with poison, but some of these other gentlemen were still alive and were making new war plans.

I opened the window. It had become dark while I had been examining the pictures and magazines. Mist was rising from the pines and it was cool.

The following day I visited the battalions. They were stationed in the area on the other side of the lake. It was not far to the lake, a quiet location in the woods. Mighty moss-covered trees grew close up to the bank.

The soldiers had erected their tents between the pines and made a bathroom using of strips of canvas. A bath!

Water was being heated in a cauldron and a sergeant major was issuing the soldiers with fresh underwear. I walked for a long time, lifting asters or creeping under them: in order not to make mistakes, I established which platoon and which company was which. Bits of uniform were hanging on the lines – trousers, caps, foot cloths. It was like being in a field camp. The soldiers were giving themselves a thorough washing and sewing on clean collars. They were writing letters.

The war was a thing of the past. Tomorrow morning they would begin training for peacetime. The officers were listening to a lecture about the end of the war and the prospects for peacetime.

I walked along the lake and discovered a second grand stone building. At both sides of the entrance stood statues of hunting dogs carved out of black stone.

On other days I went to the political department towards evening. I had been told the way. It was in the opposite direction around the lake. I had not been going long when I noticed a house in a clearing. It was covered with a half-metre-thick thatch of reeds, but the entrance was not that of an ordinary farmhouse. Only later did I discover that all the buildings here on the lake and in the wood had belonged to just one man – Göring.

As well as the political department, the divisional headquarters were also accommodated in the building with the reed roof. In a room on the ground floor, where a window took up the whole wall, a sculptor, who had been flown here from Moscow, was modelling our soldier Misha Yegorov, who had hoisted the flag on the Reichstag. He was also to model our divisional commander Shatilov.

In the studio I also looked at the well-modelled little sculpture – preliminarily made out of clay – of Pokryshkin [flying ace]. He had got his third gold star in the taking of Berlin. The sculptor pleased me. With one hand on which he was wearing a glove, the pilot showed how he had flown. The model was standing on a small table in the corner. Apparently the sculptor had brought it with him to work on.

We did not stay long in this quiet, isolated place. From this wood-land lake we soon moved across to the Ruppiner Lake near the little town of Ruppin. This was also where I spent a long time in a hospital.

And the stick? In the hospital I found the going easier when I leant on it. And when I left Germany, I took it with me. At the sanatorium in Yalta I put it in a clothes rack and forgot it. Perhaps somebody else is now using it.

CHAPTER TWENTY

At the Summer's End

I jumped down from the vehicle, the camera in my hands. I had come here to see and to photograph. For when we were fighting in Berlin there had been no time to take photographs. And there was so much that I wanted to record on film. Now I was back in Berlin and I had two extra films in my pockets.

Several months had passed since the end of the war and the summer was drawing to a close. That was why I had done everything to get some leave from the hospital. We had been released early at daybreak. At about ten o'clock we crossed the Alexanderplatz in Berlin. It was warm and sunny. I sat on the tailboard in a rickety armchair and turned my head quickly here and there. I was very calm and happy, looking for the picture to take of the passing city. Everywhere at road junctions I saw signposts nailed up, posters and pictures of our soldiers, the heroes of the fighting. The pavements were swarming with people, the businesses were open.

Unter den Linden – the Arsenal – the Humboldt University – the destroyed building of the Soviet Embassy – and then we drove through the Brandenburg Gate. In front of us the wide street stretched on through the Tiergarten, and on the right behind the trees was the Reichstag.

Our driver did not waste time looking for a suitable parking place, quickly deciding to park the vehicle at the roadside in the shade of the trees. I entered the square and with difficulty, my camera pressed to my breast, I forced my way through a crowd of people. I looked ahead and tried to find where there had been a trench and who had sheltered in it on the day when two of our battalions had taken cover before the last assault. People bumped into me, someone spoke to me, but my mind was elsewhere.

There I saw the yellow tin cans, the same cans containing meat that we once had hidden in the warm socks that our wives, grandmothers and mothers had given up knitted jackets to create. I was pushed and spoken to from all sides. Once I had seen these tins, my curiosity was aroused. I looked around and saw a man squatting with these cans on his knees.

Now I understood why these women had run up to me when I got down from the vehicle. They had expected me to sell or exchange something.

The man was pulling one can after another out of a knapsack and reached for another one and pushed it in his pocket.

Two were dealing in cigarettes.

A quite young boy perched on a tall, dead tree. He was a handsome little lad with merry eyes. I went closer. With astonishing speed he scooped up the chocolate and biscuits he was selling and quickly collected the money for them.

People were crowding round the Reichstag, in the Tiergarten and on the Charlottenburger Chaussee, and now it was obvious what was happening here. I had found myself in the black market.

I looked for the stones behind which the soldiers of my division had laid down and found cover. Many were buried among them. I had only come here for this reason and I had had no idea that I would find the square as I saw it now.

The further I went the crowds became bigger. I noticed French and British soldiers. Everyone was out to buy, sell or exchange. Germans proffered bits of clothing, items of value, knick-knacks and cameras. They took money for them but there was a preference for bread, conserves and tobacco.

I went on in the direction of the Kroll Opera House. I wanted to be alone. Suddenly a Jeep raced up and people ran to it. I had never seen such a rough-looking vehicle before. Only the framework of the construction remained, and the stuffing was coming out of the seats. While the vehicle was still moving one of the occupants jumped off. He held boxes and packets pressed to him. He called out something and vanished into the crowd.

I went on thinking that I could not buy or sell anything.

The holes and trenches over which I jumped, in which all kinds of paper lay, had been dug at a difficult time when the attack had come to a standstill. Our soldiers who had sought shelter in these positions were fired on by the Fascists in the upper levels of the Reichstag. From here, from this square, some of the soldiers fighting in front of the Reichstag had later seen the victory flag.

There was no flag on the Reichstag now.

Who would have thought that here of all places, where the dead that had fallen during the last hours of the war had been buried, should have become a black market.

I worked my way out of the crowd and found myself near the Spree. I stood on the bank. The Spree flowed past, gloomy and dirty.

I turned left, crossed a water-filled trench, and then stood in front of the building that we had called 'Himmler's House'. Our men had prepared for the attack in its cellars. This had been the last stop before the Reichstag. Now it was a ruin. The market noises did not reach as far as here.

I looked at the disfigured walls for a while, then clambered over the debris covering the pavement, knelt down and looked in the cellar. Below the window stood the boxes that our soldiers had climbed on to get out. I stood up, beating the dust off my coat and trousers. After standing at these window openings I did not need to go any further.

I went back.

An English traffic policeman with short white gaiters and white sleeve protectors was standing on a round platform. His cross straps were also white.

This was also the main entrance to the Reichstag with shot-up and damaged pillars featuring inscriptions. They would last a long time. I looked for mine, but in vain, too many new ones had been added afterwards.

I climbed up the steps uneasily. Everything that I had seen from the square was forgotten. So were the half-dark corridor and the chamber, also every room where the soldiers had stopped during the fire. Would I be able to find my way through all the vestibules, offices and many passages?

The tall entrance door was nailed shut. But I was determined to get through it. I knew that one could get into the building through the cellar window.

But I did not get through. No, it was not nailed up, but there was such a lot of dirt in front of and behind the window that I gave up.

A Soviet major, one of the army doctors came up to me, also wanting to get into the building. We finally found a small, hidden door. To all appearances we seemed to be in a part of the building that the fire had spared. Everything here had been destroyed, but we found no traces of fire. It was dark here, close and smelled musty. We wanted to get into daylight as quickly as possible.

As before it was hectic and restless in the square. Two soldiers drew the attention of the Germans and the few Soviet soldiers in the square. One was wearing a short chequered kilt and was armed with a submachine-gun. A Scottish soldier! His companion, an African, was wearing green trousers and high-laced yellow boots. They were not buying anything. They were just going through the crowd laughing heartily.

I remembered that I had wanted to take photographs, but I had carried the camera around with me for nothing. I had not thought of taking a photograph of the black market. Many wanted to drive away the misery from here and I had sympathy for them, a feeling that I had not had until now.

I wanted to get a picture of the Scottish soldier, but I did not see him again. He had vanished in the crowds. Then I thought that I would photograph one of the American soldiers, but it was as if I was cursed. An hour before the square had been swarming with people, now no one was there. Apparently they had sold their conserves and cigarettes.

I came across someone wearing dark glasses and a peaked cap surrounded by people. He seemed to be recounting something. I saw his happy, laughing face. I tried to get through to him, but people were standing around him like a wall. I used my elbows to help and said very energetically: 'A moment!'

The people moved aside with angry looks at me. I raised my camera. The American looked at me, took the cigar out of his mouth and spread out his arms. I pressed the switch. It was then I realized that he was not addressing the people, but like all the others here had been offering things for sale.

I hastened back to our one-and-a-half tonner. Soon everyone had returned and we drove off.

CHAPTER TWENTY-ONE

Our Children

Near the Reichstag is the Brandenburg Gate featuring the Quadriga. The Brandenburg Gate was badly damaged in 1945 and the Quadriga resembled a formless tangle of metal. The chariot could no longer be driven and the horses' legs were broken.

But time was passing rapidly and my daughter, born during the war in 1944, was already in the 9th Class. Yesterday she read from a German textbook, and what did I hear? That young Viktor was going to Berlin to visit Otto, a boy like himself. And the young German showed the city to his friend. They climbed aboard the S-Bahn in Alexanderplatz. (We went on foot at that time, saying the it was not too far to go.) Otto walked with his guest along the broad Unter den Linden. They saw the Brandenburg Gate, the symbol of the capital of the German Democratic Republic.

'See how it looks!' I said.

I looked at a picture of the Brandenburg Gate. It was fully restored. And above it stood the Quadriga with the galloping horses.

German children met ours, and Otto, the Young Pioneer, took Viktor to the sights of interest, showing him his city. They walked along the Unter den Linden.

CHAPTER TWENTY-TWO

Sleep in May

We had not slept for ten days, ten days and nights. We were falling asleep on our legs, only the tension keeping us upright and sometimes the schnapps.

The fighting had gone on for ten days, day and night, without a break. We had fought our way through blocked streets from building to building. Our uniforms reeked of smoke, were filthy and covered with the dust from slates and chalk. We looked like masons coming out of the roof rafters.

Then when Berlin capitulated on 2 May and things came to a standstill, we could not take another step – not even to the Brandenburg Gate. We slept! Everyone slept – soldiers and commanders – right next to the Reichstag, on the square, head to head. We slept like marmots all day long.

CHAPTER TWENTY-THREE

Aliosha

He was wounded again, and this time seriously. It had happened to him in Berlin when we had reached the Spree. It was the seventh time that he had been wounded.

They brought you to the field hospital. I saw how they had laid you on a stretcher. That was how I remember it in a farmyard near a shady red-brick wall. You were lying there in your vest without your field blouse. The field blouses had been taken from the wounded. One hand hung down from the stretcher. I felt compelled to look at it. The sleeve was rolled up and I noticed the scars of two wounds. One wound was above the elbow, the other below. They were old scars.

You had been thickly bandaged and were waiting for a vehicle. You were very pale, lying there with your eyes closed.

I thought about all our encounters, especially the first one. Where had you come from to join us? Shortly before being transferred I myself had been in the Baltic on that then quiet sector of the front.

The vehicle arrived. You were lifted up, not by medical orderlies – there were none there – but by two of your soldiers.

Your opened your eyes and smiled. You saw me and tried to wave with your dangling hand. You moved yourself a little, not wanting to do more. So I said goodbye to you.

You were driven off but your whistle remained behind. I took it with me.

I am writing these lines like a letter to you. Perhaps you are alive and will read it when it is published.

We met at the foot of the Black Heights, so memorable to us. For a long time I had wanted to get to the forward trenches. The place where I was standing lay deep and marshy. I had had an arduous time, getting through the willow and alder bushes. Suddenly I was standing in a trench. It was quieter in the wood than in the field, although the enemy were nearer. The soldiers here were not as alert as elsewhere.

A soldier showed me the way to the commander. I went along a narrow, crumbling communications trench. Bent double, I climbed into a half-finished command post. Although heaps of freshly dug clay lay around, the construction work was well underway.

You were hacking at the hard ground with a hatchet and did not see me. You were then only wearing a vest. Your field blouse, the epaulettes of which each had a small star, was lying in a corner.

'How come you are doing this yourself?' I wondered that you, the platoon commander, was digging out the command post.

'We only have a few soldiers left and have to maintain a defence' was your reply, and you sat down on a ledge that would be your bed. Breathing heavily from the strenuous work, you drew on a cigarette. Your fingers did not do what you wanted them to.

It was quite bright in the command post, but I felt my hair standing on end. His was the colour of pale straw, at least that was the impression.

You lit a cigarette, took a deep breath and bent down, your elbows on your well-spread knees. Now I could see you better and established that your hair was not straw blonde or ash coloured, like the time of year. And although it was clear what colour your hair was, I asked you: 'Your hair is white?'

'Yes', you said simply. You must have answered this question many times.

Before you had been called up you had worked in an armaments factory in Tula. You became a soldier in 1942.

That was a bad year. You recounted that you were stuck in one firetrap after another. The earth was rocked by explosions. Shells exploded 2m away. You were unable to dig in. If you lifted a hand, it was torn to shreds. You showed me how the German aircraft circled over you with howling sirens as you crawled in the grass.

Things intensifed so much each time, as if the fighting that you had already endured had become worse, and you would not forget it to your dying day. But new heavy fighting was yet to come.

You participated in vigorous reconnaissance, jumped into an enemy trench and grabbed a 'tongue' [prisoner]. And that didn't just happen once. It repeated itself often ... like everything.

Your hair turned white in Stalingrad. At first it was only a few hairs: your comrades noticed this. You did not want people to see it and tried to hide it.

I can still see you clearly before me today, see you in the half-finished command post, see your white hair.

Naturally I had heard and read that hair can turn white overnight. But I had not really believed it. You were so young, very young, perhaps 19 or 20 years old.

On another occasion you told me how you had been given leave after a stay in hospital and went home to Danilovka near Tula. You appeared in the village, wet, soaked through, with your cap pulled down on your neck. Your sister saw you through a window. You climbed up the steps and came towards you calling: 'Lionka is here!'

How small the house seemed! Your mother was also there. She had turned towards you, hesitant, one step more ...

You pulled off your coat, and removed your cap.

Your sister cried out: 'Lionka, what is that?'

But your mother said: 'See, he has turned white.' And she pulled your head to her. She was smaller than you and dark haired.

That evening the youngsters collected around you at home. You sat among them, among friends. And you sat as bent forward as in the command post. And you spoke quietly as one talks when the enemy is only a few metres away crouching in another trench.

One of your friends said: 'Liosha, shave off your hair, perhaps it will grow differently.'

'Alexei, colour your hair', said a girl.

But your mother looked determinedly at the children and said: 'You should stay as you are.'

We then left the dugout, which had become narrow and damp. The snow was melting. The willow branches glimmered a bluish red. We breathed in the clean air deeply. The snow was melting everywhere. We went on past a garden littered with broken toys. But there were no children there.

Where we had come through! Through how many villages of which only the names, only the chimneys remained, positions, trenches, wherever one looked.

I came back to you on the Oder. Yes on the Oder, Aliosha! That is how far you had forced your way forward! Our troops were standing in Rumania and on the borders of Czechoslovakia. Our divisions were deployed here. We knew that the Germans had prepared a strong defence here on the Oder.

You were already a captain. We had not seen each other for a long time. But I knew all about you. You had participated in many battles and were now commanding a company. There were many decorations on your field blouse. You were more mature, older. But you still had

the sunburnt reddish face of a boy. You had become a good commander. The soldiers loved you. You were quiet and kind, but could
also be scornful. That became clear to me in the two days I spent with
you.

You no longer lived with your soldiers in a dugout, but in a house,
on the first floor of a big house. The soldiers had occupied a large
room, but we lived together in a small room.

Over your bed hung an embroidered cloth, apparently a souvenir, a
family motto or a psalm. Close to it on a nail you had hung a black
whistle.

'Your runner?' I pointed to the whistle.

'You bet', you replied. And your broad, strong face turned into a
smile. You said that you had had it for two years, and were happy with
it. This whistle helped you a lot. When machine-pistols clattered, if a
shell exploded nearby, orders could not be heard. You can shout as
loud as you like, but nobody hears. However, the whistle ...

I moved into a long, narrow trench with low breastworks, and there
I saw you and your soldiers. At 20 years old, which you became in the
spring when I got to know you, in a heavy grey greatcoat and a faded
cap.

As I write this, I too have gone grey. Have so many years passed
already?

It is as if we had only got to know each other yesterday.

'Eagle, get ready', you said. Eagle is what you called your soldiers.
You prepare yourself with your feet ready to jump as foreseen for this
purpose, waiting for the signal to jump over the breastwork and storm
forwards on the other trench opposite in which the enemy is sitting.

And I hear the signal, I hear the whistle, your whistle, Aliosha,
which I still have today. And whenever I see you, I have the commander with the face of a boy and white hair before my eyes, giving
the signal for the attack.

CHAPTER TWENTY-FOUR

Volodya's Poem

During the war years the newspapers published many stories. Their publishers told me how many kilometres there were still to go to Berlin, how they fought and much more.

The war was over. Everyone had waited for it and yet the victory seemed to have come as a surprise. The poets were silent. I read only one poem in our army newspaper on 9 May.

Perhaps I should not begin my account with this memory, but the poem stuck in my mind because it was the only one, and because Vladimir Savizki had published it. He was the editor of the army newspaper, and I of the divisional newspaper. For a journalist he was still younger than myself. I had come to the newspaper a year before the end of the war, he half a year after me. We had both been taken from the ranks – I had previously been a tank soldier, he had commanded a battery.

Soon after joining the newspaper a poem had come into my hands. It came from a young girl. I was told that a gunner had written the verses and that he was now lying in an army hospital. In the neighbouring bed was a lieutenant, a company commander, who once while reading the newspaper had turned his head and said: 'Look Comrade Senior Lieutenant, he writes an astonishing poem and has apparently not yet seen a Fascist.'

'Let me see', Savizki said.

The verse in the newspaper had been written by him.

Our first encounter occurred as follows. I had come back from the front line, had thrown off my half pelt and sat down at the table. The driver Mitya had placed a bowl of steaming soup in front of me. I had not slept for two nights, was tired and that was apparently why I did not notice the new chap sat at the table.

'We have a guest. Introduce yourself. This is Savizki', someone said to me.

I saw a stocky 30-year-old and, on first impression, no longer a young man. His short hair was combed to one side, his broad face appearing somewhat symmetrical. I saw his upright forehead and his rather small mouth.

He had already participated in many things, he knew defence and retreat, and had taken part in an operation behind the enemy lines. In this action his platoon had lost almost all its guns. He was badly wounded and almost written off.

His reading and his knowledge astounded me. I had read little at first. Moreover I had completed a course at an institute before the war and became an engineer. On the other hand I had not attended the Communist Party schools at all. It was no longer necessary other than to listen to him. In a short while we became friends. Before going to a unit I would look for Savizki, even if I had to go 5 or 6km.

Apparently I was almost an author in his eyes because I worked on the newspaper. I was an admirer of his and was even a bit shy in his presence. He was a soldier, a front-line officer, a brave man and a poet. I admired him, as boys admire heroes. He always had a new verse. He would read to me with his deep, somewhat dull voice. The poems were half documentary. They contained what only one could know who was constantly under fire in the trenches on a daily basis.

He was the first poet that I got to know and although in a sense I was his teacher, I observed the essence of poetry for the first time. My admiration for him was so great that I felt the desire to write like him – apparently about only what one had actually seen.

'How is it with Savizki?' I was asked in the office whenever I returned.

'Still in the right direction,' I replied. His battery shot mainly directly ahead.

Our second encounter took place near Nevel. We were going through a wood in the winter night and reciting poetry – our own and others, everything that we knew. Unfortunately that wasn't not much.

Then we met once more in the spring. The snow was melting away. Volodia had his uniform cap on and was wearing waterproof boots. However, his battery was not in action. He had established his dugout under a house right on the street. The house was in a destroyed village. The petroleum lamp burned brightly on the homemade table. Our shadows danced on the walls. The soldiers were very discreet. We hardly noticed them. They knew the poems as if they had written them themselves, but they didn't act as if they weren't listening as their commander read this poem by an unknown lieutenant from the booklet. I now have a poem from Volodia in my head about an old man. He returns to his house, tears a German newspaper off the wall with a trembling hand and reveals Lenin's picture under it. We each drank 100g, perhaps even 300g and talked a lot that night, not far from the growling guns.

I slept on a camp bed. Volodia wanted to lie down later. I woke up several times and saw him sitting over his booklet. Towards morning Volodia read me his poem: 'a shot flew through the door into the dugout and exploded near us ...'.

Sometime later this really happened. A shell hit the dugout. The soldiers had a job digging their commander out.

That happened near Sebesh. When I heard about it I immediately hastened to his battery. But I did not find Savizki, nor was he in the field dressing station. Next day an old driver brought him to us.

Savizki did not want to be evacuated to the rear area. We settled him in a hayloft. He was not at all well, his hearing was badly affected and he could only speak with difficulty.

I climbed up to him in the hayloft and 'cured' him with milk. His condition slowly improved. Within a week he was asking for paper. Here in the hayloft of a wealthy Latvian he wrote his poem about an artilleryman. We published it later in our newspaper.

He was desperate to return to his battery, although he was not fit for action. But one day a vehicle arrived and took Volodia away. He had been assigned to our 3rd Shock Army's newspaper.

On the morning of 9 May – it was a sunny morning and the day promised to be hot – our companies, battalions and regiments assembled throughout the streets of Berlin.

During the night the announcement about the end of the war was issued and no one had slept. The minutes during which the order was read out to the troops were no less exciting. Everything came at once – joy, triumph, tears.

I went to the 674th Regiment which had participated in the taking of the Reichstag. And naturally Volodia came too from the printing shop of this regiment, which was his regiment, to his battery, to his soldiers. Many of his faithful comrades had been killed.

CHAPTER TWENTY-FIVE

Soldier and Singer

This is my first recollection of him. Our truck was standing in a village near Kalinin. I was sitting in the cab, having placed a board over the steering wheel, and he was plodding through the deep snow ahead of the truck. He was wearing a shabby padded jacket. His face looked tired, his lips drawn. He was moving them, but I could not understand what he was saying. He kept on speaking ahead of himself while he went to and fro over the ground, thus ensuring that he did not step in his old footsteps, avoiding the trampled path.

He seemed to be having difficulty in finding his way. The snow was deep and one foot immediately sank in whenever he pulled out the other.

In my mind I still see the deeply overhanging straw roof of the stall, the tall snowdrifts, everything that I saw through the driver's windscreen. When he walked back to me, I opened the door and he showed me the beginning of a poem.

The village was called Denissova. I was there for one or two days in a simple farmhouse, one corner of the room divided off by a tent sheet. A big Russian stove stood in the middle. Black painted wooden boxes were stacked at the window. They were already known to me as typeset cases. This was our print shop's accommodation.

On our way here we had crossed over a frozen lake. On the banks stood the village houses with their windows facing the water. Our print shop was situated on the outskirts.

This was my first command. Previously I had worked for about a month at the army's newspaper. Apparently they had wanted to assess me. I had only visited army units twice, and now I was posted to the divisional newspaper.

I first got to know Loboda here. He had dark hair and dark skin. He only had the first two stripes on his shoulder straps. His field blouse was old and thin, but his trousers were padded and thick.

The day after my arrival he escorted me to the divisional and regimental headquarters. We met the battalions and split up to go to the companies, returning together that evening to the print shop.

I had heard of Loboda before I got to know him personally. I had read his poems in the newspaper.

We remained together for the winter and part of the summer of 1944. Later too, after he had been transferred to an artillery regiment, right up until the day and hour that I found him in a hospital tent.

Today when I leaf through the yellowed pages of the old newspapers I can still find his sketches and poems. Exactly like us, he wrote poems, reports and also pamphlets, anything required. Loboda was well known in the division. We sang the song that he had published. It was the division's song.

Within the small group responsible for the divisional newspaper here was a soldier who understood writing, a valuable associate. Loboda knew how to mould the material required for a divisional newspaper. He very quickly became proficient in all areas of writing for the newspaper.

Loboda was born in Kiev in 1915 at Pavlovskaya 10. He had worked at a wagon factory in Mytishtshi. He published in the *Pionerskaya Pravda* and the Leningrad *Kostyor*, studied at the Literary Institute and at the beginning of the war was working for a radio station. He censored the letters to the front – there is still such a system in place now. But then in 1941 he went off to the front as a machine-gunner. He was a decisive and determined person.

Sometimes we spent the night out in a tent in the snow, in a canyon or on a river bank. He wrote, despite the cold, and not just reports and informative pieces, which we were obliged to do, but also poetry. He had the makings of a great poet.

I was now looking at our old divisional newspaper and discovered that many articles and sketches were signed with his name. The heroes of his reports were Malyuk, Shayachmetov, Tshemankin, Netshayev and Gerassimov. Many leaflets bear his name.

Sometimes we spent the whole day together preparing material. He worked quickly to get as much done as possible in daylight. Our desks, which were homemade, stood in opposite corners of the truck. We hardly spoke a word while we were working.

Most of the time we also lived together. Once we had a very big dugout. We tried heating it up by burning wood, but without success. But we could not worry about the cold, we had reports to write. On the day that Loboda's friend fell, the Komsomol organizer Sascha Michanov, he dedicated a column to him. Loboda sat up the whole night and wrote a poem.

When were we not usually together! But my recollections always focus on the publishing and I want to tell you about it here. The following event gave me pleasure.

Two of the division's battalions had crossed a river and formed a bridgehead. Loboda and I crouched in a foxhole close to the river not far from the crossing point. The foxhole in which we had sought shelter was so narrow that there was hardly enough room for one. In addition to this, it was positioned low down and water had penetrated the hole.

Fascist aircraft were attacking us in waves. We stood it out for two days at this bridgehead but all was in vain. The troops went into the attack and our material, which was concerned with the defence, was no longer required. Articles were wanted about the attack.

Then Loboda was suddenly transferred overnight. This was a surprise for us working on the newspaper. We were told that there was no other alternative. This was an unscheduled move and neither pleas nor proposals made any difference.

In his place came another equally unscheduled replacement.

Until then I had never been in an artillery regiment. Now Loboda was there, I went to see him. In the morning we visited the firing positions. We stood in a covered trench that was deep and capacious. We saw a church nearby. There was a barn near the trench. The level ground around was covered in grass.

The sun was standing high in the sky and it was hot. We had our elbows propped up on the breastwork. Each of us was reading a book. One was Remarque's *All Quiet on the Western Front*, the other a book of poetry. Loboda had got the poetry together from somewhere or other. I had found Remarque's novel lying about. It made no special impression on me, although I had been moved by it before the war.

Now I had all of it in front of me; a trench, exploding shells and bodies bloated by the heat in no-man's-land.

The situation ensured the silent verses had a much greater effect upon us. Perhaps this suited us better because they did not speak of the war, because the life that we led was so violent and less meaningful than what was expressed in these poems.

Loboda often wrote to his mother, who lived in Moscow, asking her to look out for his poems.

These poems have been preserved. In them is his voice, the voice of a soldier from the bank of the Lovatj.

At this time he also wrote a poem about how after many, many years the grey-haired mother sought the distant traces of her son. She found her son's grave in the land where he had fought.

But death did not overtake Loboda in this trench, where we stood with books in our hands, but rather on a hillside in Kurland as his regiment rose from the bridgehead at Ajviekst. He led the breakthrough offensive over the Latvian border through towns to the shores of the Bay of Riga. As the enemy's second and third defensive lines were taken, so everything started to move, the rear services and also the headquarter staffs.

The Baltic Levels spread before them. Only close to the sea can the earth be so level.

The regiments' rear services had not dispersed when I arrived. They were located in a wood.

Everywhere lay gas-mask containers, shreds of paper and notebooks. Many people kept a diary in this war.

My name was called. A girl came up to me and pointed at a tent. She said: 'Loboda is lying there.'

I went into the tent and almost stumbled over his legs. It was a small tent, the canvas allowing little light in. He was lying face down on the earth. I recognized him, kneeled down and pulled him up.

His face was puffy. His head was bandaged, but the blood was trickling through the dressing. I put my hand on his shoulder and called him. He did not answer, groaned slightly, barely audible. Or was he whispering something?

He had been hit by a stray bullet. He had gone over this field in his cape, which the wind billowed out, and had suddenly sunk to the ground.

Shattered, I left the tent and jumped on the running board of a passing truck. We drove over a field and crossed the trenches on the planks that had been placed over them. German soldiers lay buried in these trenches.

The advance continued. The Fascist troops were unable to stand up to our attack. We pushed forward and no one could stop us.

Loboda is buried in Dobel where the field hospital was located. He did not die on the day that I was there. He was taken to a hospital, although those in the field hospital were of the opinion that it was a hopeless case. He did not regain consciousness. His manuscripts, notebooks and poems were stuck in a haversack that was lost and never found again.

My friend Loboda did not live to see the Day of Victory. He never got to Riga and fell on 18 October 1944 during the breaching of the defences of the Ajviekste in Latvia.

Now he lies buried and does not know that his friends and the heroes of his poetry – the soldiers of the division in which he served – got to Berlin and climbed the steps of the Reichstag.

The soldier and singer Loboda. Pines keep watch over his grave at Ajviekste.

I summon a taxi. I had had this idea just a moment before. We soon stopped before a big house in a narrow Moscow lane where I had never been before.

Naturally much time had passed, but nevertheless I was afraid of reopening old wounds. I climbed out and went up in the lift. A woman opened it for me. I saw immediately that this was Loboda's mother.

His picture hung on a wall showing him as a sergeant, and looking at me from this picture was my friend of twelve years ago.

CHAPTER TWENTY-SIX

The Youth

In the winter of 1943 a large, gaunt soldier came to the publishing truck of our army newspaper. One says it this way – soldier – but he was an officer, a lieutenant. Even a layman would have known that he had not been a lieutenant for long. He had been wearing those little stars on his shoulder straps for two weeks at the most.

He was wearing a half fur, perhaps even a greatcoat. It was so long ago that I cannot say with certainty. A map case hung over his shoulder and inside, apart for the map and a handkerchief, was also a book of poems. The poems were written in impressive, lively handwriting. I remember it exactly. I was then also a lieutenant and had already published my first poems. I was only making a brief visit to the army newspaper.

The officer introduced himself. He was called Lessin, Alexander Lessin, and he gave us his poems. We published some of them.

In the course of one-and-a-half years we met sometimes on a narrow path, sometimes between chimneys rising out of the snow. Our divisions lay near each other and who should meet here on the ways to the front if not us, the correspondents of the divisional newspaper. One was going forward on an assignment, the other was going straight back. The one with the snow-white camouflage cape went forwards and the one with the dirty, scorched one was going back.

Once Alexander came to see me when I had just received a letter informing me that my father had fallen. We sat on the wing of a vehicle and my friend tried to comfort me.

At that time I was already with the army newspaper. Often it was not easy for us. We had to go to and fro between the units. We were obliged to write everything – articles, sketches, reports, poems and also cheerful things, even when one was in no mood for jokes.

My friend had it worse than I did. Before he turned up at the publishing truck he had been a soldier in a rifle company. With us he found an unexpected protector; the head of the political department, an old Communist, who noticed this nimble and skilful colleague, and was obviously proud of his poet. But Alexander was only well tempered and patient at the beginning, but then he mutinied. It was easier for him to subordinate himself among the fighting troops. He found this difficult with the publishing team. It happened that, in order not to be disturbed at his work, the editor had a sentry posted in front of his door to prevent anyone from entering. So my friend ran with his rucksack over his shoulder to the dugout of the political department and tried to get the leader to have him transferred to another unit, preferably to a fighting one.

'What, have you been quarrelling again?' asked the head of the political department. Then when he saw the dark face of the lieutenant, he said: 'It doesn't matter, don't get upset! That is not important! There is room here for you too. Stay here and write your stuff here. Write your poems.'

The editor came very quickly.

The newspaper came out only every second day, but no one had time to set it out. And then the editor put a stop to it and said that the lieutenant had to return to the publishing team.

'What is he supposed to do for you?' asked the colonel. 'You handle him badly ... and with me he can write in peace'. And after a look at the bewildered editor he went on: 'You chase him with a cudgel and expect him to sing like a nightingale.'

I recall that Alexander went to Moscow one day. Soon afterwards his poems appeared in newspapers and in an omnibus volume. He wrote me a letter from Moscow in which there was talk of long-haired, spectacle-wearing youths with little experience who had yet to join the fighting, but who 'stuttered in strange accents'. This letter reached me at the little Ajviekste River in Latvia on the second day of the battle of the bridgehead.

Finally we are both standing at the Brandenburg Gate. Because we knew that we must soon part, we exchanged addresses, although neither of us had a permanent residence.

We had met in the Reichstag the day before on a narrow dilapidated stair that led to the roof. One was coming down and the other was going up.

We met again a year later in the Crimea. It was warm there and we had come to settle. We were young, critical and cantankerous.

Now he had sent me his latest book. It is called *Unrest*. That suits him. He is always trying to create expressive titles. He rejects the suggestions of his friends, who try to get him to use quiet, soothing language: his favourite words are 'Wind', 'Storm'.

His book contains many war poems, poems about his and my youth.

When we met in the Crimea we recalled how we had bumped into each other climbing to the roof of the Reichstag. My friend declared that he had then held the model of the Reichstag building in his hands. I maintained that, to the contrary, it had only been two plaster of Paris pillars.

Comrades had found the model and shown it to him. He had broken off two pillars and held them in his hand as we viewed the city spreading out beneath us. A bit of wire protruded from the plaster pillars. And we have been arguing for fifteen years about what actually happened.

CHAPTER TWENTY-SEVEN

My Brother

I had a brother. He was really my cousin, but he was more than a brother to me.

We grew up in a Siberian village on the far side of the Urals. We ran together in the woods, caught fish together from a sandbank in the river, and we slept under a sheepskin, lying on an oven. When we started school we sat next to each other. Many took us for brothers.

Hardly grown, we put on field blouses and were very proud of it. By chance I acquired an old military overcoat and was happy! We were Red Army men like our fathers and prepared to die for our convictions.

We volunteered for the army early. At the railway station, the collecting point, we sat down with our sacks before driving off in a military train. We were both sent to the western border, where some of the wagons were decoupled at a large railway station that was full of trains. We were to be taken to Poltava. Here we said farewell. Our comrades, boys from all over the country, surrounded us: 'Look, those are two brothers saying goodbye to each other!'

That was in the winter of 1940. The war began six months later.

He fell in 1942 at Layby 564 in the big battle on the Volga. That was at the time when tanks were attacking tanks. Later his parents received letters from soldiers of the company that he had led in the attack. He had been their deputy political adviser. We had both dreamed of this earlier. I had read his letter from the loophole in the tank and envied him.

We two – him and I – were 20 years old then.

I travel to the place where he died several years after the Victory Salute had thundered in Berlin. The Volga–Dom Canal had been completed on the barren Volga Steppe, and now it was about to be opened.

CHAPTER TWENTY-EIGHT

After the Arrival

We had last seen each other at Karinhall, Göring's country residence on the Schorfheide. Years had passed since then.

One day I found myself going home. It was very late. From a distance I saw that no light was burning in our house. That was unusual. My wife always waited for me, even when I came home very late. It was quiet, no breath of air, both my feet moved unwillingly.

Lanterns were burning at the railway station, but their light did not reach me. When I left the station on the way to the village the night seemed darker. Although I knew the way, I went carefully through the darkness in order to stay on the narrow beaten track.

I crossed the stream on the swaying bridge of two wooden planks that were not yet frozen, despite the frost. The village was asleep, the lights in the houses extinguished. The steps to my house creaked like the footbridge over the stream. The boughs of the white willow hung motionless over the steps.

The door was frozen fast again. No wonder – when a house is heated badly the door freezes fast. Usually I help my wife with the stove. She then pushes against the door. Today I will have to see to it myself. I lean my bag packed full of heavy books against the house wall. I push against the door with both hands, rattle and shake, and eventually the door opens.

There is no one in the kitchen, but a weak light comes from under the gap in the door. I am puzzled, for I had thought my wife was already asleep. As I enter the room, I see a man. The light blinds me, my eyes not yet adjusted from the darkness.

A man stands up, steps towards me and then I recognize him. Neustroyev.

We sit on the bed in which his little son, Jura, is sleeping. Everything was so unusual. We last saw each other on the Schorfheide a few weeks after the fighting in Berlin had ceased. It had been a warm, summer-like day. Now it was winter – winter 1957. How many winters had passed since then? Twelve? Really twelve?

He had looked for me in Simferopol in the Crimea, but for some time I had been living here in a village near Moscow, about 20km from the city.

It was cold here. The youngster lay half dressed in the bed. We occupied one room in this house, which was used by the owner as a summer house and unheated. The only source of heat was the petrol cooker, but it needed a lot of fuel and we had to go to the railway station if we wanted to buy petrol.

Then my wife arrived. Despite the late hour she had gone into the village and got some beer. There was nothing else.

We sat at the table. I drank but my friend did not. He drank only yoghurt. We decided to leave all serious talk until the next day. For the moment the fact that we were sitting next to each other was the most important thing for us.

He was wearing a grey suit with a tie. But meanwhile twelve winters had passed.

He seemed disappointed with my accommodation, the cold walls and the lack of furniture. Looking at him I could see that he had not expected this.

The youngster woke up, believed that he had missed something important and was sulky. He had wanted to be with us when we met. He knew which soldier had lain behind which stone on the Königsplatz in Berlin. He knew everything just as if he had been with us.

We went to bed, wanting to get up early the next day. Neustroyev wanted to go to Moscow.

'Come with me,' he said, 'show me everything.' I gladly accepted his invitation.

The next day he paced up and down the room smoking and talked excitedly about the first failed attack on the Reichstag. His memory of all the details was vivid: the fighting for the bridge, on the square, the storming of the entrance.

We missed the train but still managed to get to Moscow as we had planned. Then we went through the snow-covered city with our noses hidden in our scarves.

We visited the Army Museum. It was a long time since I had last been there. We handed in our hats and coats at the cloakroom, and then went into the first room.

Suddenly a comrade stopped us. He wanted to see our tickets. We had none. We had forgotten that this was a museum and that one required tickets. We were taken to the director's room. A long conversation ensued. But Jura became bored and was burning to go round the rooms that we had passed on the way.

He pulled me by the hand and we left the room. Jura said that he did not want to look at the photographs but rather the equipment and mortars. Finally he recalled why we had come here.

'Where is it?' he asked. And he meant the Victory Flag.

A group of visitors was standing there listening attentively to a young girl leading and briefing the group. We joined them.

'And to protect them we keep them under glass. Everything is being done to maintain them longer.'

In the days when they flew over the Reichstag they were brighter. They had faded over the years. They had been handed over to the soldiers without inscriptions, but now they bore the divisional badge.

'That is it, Jura!'

'Uncle Vasya, lift me up.'

I lifted him up so that he could see them better. He looked at them for a long time, then said wonderingly: 'They look just like every other flag.'

The young museum guide informed the visitors standing around her where the flags had been hoisted. The girl's explanation was not quite accurate, but she spoke very solemnly. Jura discovered that on major special occasions the flags were taken to the Kremlin.

There was a picture on the pedestal by the flags. One was of a small group of officers. One of these was Jura's father, and the son, standing in front of me, looked surprisingly similar.

'Do you know where this battalion commander is now?' someone said, pointing to Jura's father.

The girl did not know. I wanted to be able to lift up Jura and say that he was the son of the battalion commander, but I did not do that. Then Jura pointed at the picture with his finger and said: 'That is Papa.'

Everyone looked at him. The similarity was unmistakable.

'He is here and is coming', I said.

Neustroyev came to the front and then stood near the flag. The museum director approached him and suggested: 'He can tell us a little about it.'

The girl gave him a pointer. He grasped it as if it was his salvation and went to the model of the Reichstag. He was pale and from that I realized that he was very agitated.

'That is the building', he said and took a step closer. He was finding it difficult to talk. Then he took a deep breath as if he was struggling for the right words. 'Our brave soldiers occupied it on 30 April 1945.'

Embarrassed, he looked at the pointer as if deliberating how his hands should act, and he smiled to himself.

'In short, comrades,' he continued, now in an assured tone, 'that is the building.'

And he recounted how his battalion stormed the Reichstag, how the soldiers fought within the Reichstag and how they hoisted their victory flags.

It had become quiet in the big room. Unnoticed, new visitors pushed their way in. Photographers – they are almost always there at the right moment – wanted to photograph him. The picture should show the father showing the victory flags to his son. Jura complied patiently with all their requests. He raised his head, he lowered his head, the little hand somewhat higher, the foot a little back. Finally he had had enough and made his way over to the guns. Jura's father stood before the glass display case and looked at the flags as if he was looking at them for the first time. On the floor lay flags and standards of the conquered Fascists. On one flag the material was blackened and full of holes. He went up close to it, stood on tiptoe and said quietly: 'This is the way it looks now!'

CHAPTER TWENTY-NINE

That's Us!

All of Moscow seemed to be at the exhibition of Czechoslovakian glass!

We wandered through the dark, black shrouded rooms enjoying the drawings and the fine polishied objects I stood in the vestibule at a table with pictures on. They showed a sitting of the national assembly and the chimneys of factories under construction. Beneath these was an old, dim photograph. It was of a hazy street in old Prague and a Soviet tank densely packed with our soldiers. It was rolling along, surrounded by people. Their uniforms were dirty and covered in dust, but our soldiers sat there still and concentrating.

We are on this rumbling tank in the Czechoslovakian capital. But the faces, the faces – they are happy and tired and glowing with joy. And the eyes look thoughtful. There is a boy, a young soldier who has a face that could have come from an icon. All these soldiers that are making their way through Prague in the middle of the celebrating, excited crowd remain silent and strong like the youngster. We must have looked just like this in Berlin. Among our soldiers sits a local man wearing a hat. He is just as unkempt as our soldiers, but happy.

And people, how many people, how many eyes!

I recall how I myself once stopped in a little Polish town among the people whom we had come to help. I stood there for many hours.

Strong snow and rain started to pelt my face. But I stood and stood observing the tanks crashing through the streets, looking at the passing vehicles and the infantry ...

From the crowd I look around at our Soviet Army, at my comrades. That was unforgettable. I stood and saw that I was myself a drop, a drop of rain in a stream – I was part of the army, I was a piece of the mass, I was a fragment of this living avalanche ... Then I saw myself as though for the first time.

Perhaps this was the first time. How dusty we were then and how faded our blouses were. We did not want to go to a parade, we were fighting a war. We wore short coats and puttees, we were tired and sweated through, but strong. Yes, perhaps we were tired, but we did not notice the fatigue then, we did not think about it. We were warriors.

CHAPTER THIRTY

The Loyalty of a Friend

A few years ago I received an unexpected letter, a letter from Nikolai Belyayev. He had written to the publishers of the *Orgoniok*. A poem of mine was being published. He was enquiring about me.

I replied to him that I had not forgotten anything, that I remembered everything. But either I had not been given his address correctly, or he was no longer there, in any case I received no reply to my letter.

We had not seen each other since our time in Berlin. Then the soldiers of the Assault Company recognized him immediately in the dark corridors of the Reichstag – the young officer, the lieutenant in the big heavy boots. He was wearing a reddish field blouse, the collar of which he had hacked off. Pistols hung on his hips. His brows and temples were covered in dust and looked white.

In each regiment and in each company I had an officer – mainly deputy political advisers – that I sought out first to go into the units with. Kolya had often accompanied me, the divisional correspondent, on my quick, brief visits during the last year of the war. He always knew which company we should go to and how best to get to it. He knew exactly where his regiment was stationed – between the Twer Lakes or the hills – in whatever area and whatever order of battle. Kolya understood my suggestions and led me to those that I should speak to and introduced me.

Later too, when we found ourselves in Poland and then in Germany, he led me into the foremost positions on several occasions.

While I took my home-made notebook out of my map case and questioned a machine-gunner about how the night in this sector and his firing sector were, Kolya would chat with a member of the Komsomol Office, or with a soldier with no front-line experience who had come from the reserve. Often, however, he would summon the soldiers around me and give them the Army Report and brief them on other military matters. And on hot days, if an attack was being organized, he would prepare leaflets.

Kolya came from the Kalinin area. Before the war he had worked at the Komsomol district committee in Peno. But I will return to this later.

Kolya did not speak about himself. As I approached a dugout once I heard his voice. I stepped closer and stayed standing at the door. He was talking about the Kalinin partisans, especially about Lisa Tchaikina.

I stayed until he stopped talking. Then we went back to the headquarters, to his dugout. He had neither an orderly nor a runner. He heated the stove himself, which he had to if he was going to spend the night there.

Once we had layed down and covered ourselves with the blanket, I confessed that I had eavesdropped on him. And then he told me that Lisa came from his home town and had even been a classmate of his. They had known each other since they were small.

Kolya remembered a small, welcoming room. Lisa sat at the secretary's red, cloth-covered table. Next to it stood the desk of the deputy secretary, Kolya. Things were lively at the district committee with young people coming in from the Kolchoses, schools and woodwork shops.

Kolya then discovered from the newspapers that Lisa had become a partisan. Once the Germans had been driven back, Peno and the villages in the neighbourhood were visited by the partisans. Lisa too went from village to village. She went into the houses and told them that Moscow lived and that liberation was not far away.

By the time I got to know Kolya at the front, Peno had long been liberated. He had taken leave from his unit and gone there. The place had very much changed meanwhile and the park had been cut down.

Kolya found Marusia, Lisa's older sister. She was working in a print shop. Marusia told him what torments Lisa had been put through, how they had led her into a snowdrift and shot her at the pump house.

I told Kolya to write all this down and, when I came back to him again, he handed me his sketches. One could see how focused he had been making them, and what trouble he had taken. Many had been revised several times.

Lisa was buried in Peno on the woodland road. The grave had no memorial, only a cross of young fir branches lay on it.

The front was already a long way from Peno. Almost three years had passed since Kolya had left the Komsomol district committee to go to the front.

When I met Kolya in the Reichstag again, I immediately recognized him. I had gone astray down a rubble-strewn corridor and he came towards me. I only recognized him when he came into the light. He was wearing his reddish field blouse and spotted boots. His light-coloured hair and brows were so dusty that they looked white. He held a wad of newspapers in each of his hands. He wanted to go to the soldiers who were in the cellars in which the Fascists had been sitting only the day before. Far away was Peno, the little town at the mouth of the Volga. A memorial stone to Lisa had been set up in the newly planted woodland park. As Kolya recounted the first night of peace that we spent in the Reichstag, I recalled that I had read the name of Lisa Tchaikina on one of the shot-up pillars of the Reichstag. Oddly enough, I had not realized that Kolya Belyayev had written the name of his school comrade, the secretary of the district council, the name of the girl Lisa, on the Reichstag.

CHAPTER THIRTY-ONE

There – In the Village

Actually I wanted to visit the survivors, but had gone about it in such a way that I had to fly to them at their homes, to their families. I had previously visited Kantara, Berest and Bulatov. But I was flying to a Bryansk village, to Pyatnizki's wife, to his son. We often thought of him.

It was like this too at our meeting in Moscow. There was no one who hadn't thought of them. The aircraft I flew in rocked and my seat was hard. I was surrounded by boxes and bundles.

I had a picture of Pyatnizki with me. It had been sent to me from the village only that day, apparently having hung on a wall until then. Aside from this, I had some letters with me that had been handed to me by the publishers.

From the picture he really looked as Neustroyev had described him. 'Women did not find him good looking, but he was a soldier – just as one sees in books!'

I have received many letters after my account of Pyatnizki was published in *Pravda*, many letters. One was from Perm. The former gunner and scout of the 328th Artillery Regiment A. Shipilovski wrote:

I also had the opportunity of taking part in storming the Reichstag in the same division. But that is not the point. I will only say something about the heroism of Pyotr Pyatnizki. When the attack began there was a soldier in front with a red cloth. He ran to the main entrance and up the steps to the columns. Then the red cloth vanished behind the columns. There was some frenzied fighting and observation was difficult because of the explosions. The soldiers were so inspired that everyone followed.

I thought about the picture again.

The comrades only knew that he was of medium size and had had sharply protruding back bones. Also they had not forgotten his speed. We sat down on a stone at the side of the dilapidated road near Schneidemuhl and I questioned him. During the night he had put his machine-gun into position at a crossroads and taken on the Fascists as they tried to break out of Schneidemuhl. Apparently he had been decorated with a medal for bravery after this battle.

He looked strong in the picture. It is the face of a soldier at war.

Pyatnizki had taken part in the first one-and-a-half years of the war and had proved himself. In 1944 he joined us in the 150th Division as a machine-gunner. How he had fought!

Among the letters was also one from Achtyrka.

In your published article you mention the name of a soldier known to me, or a namesake of his. Apparently Pyatnizki was wounded in the chest in the attack on the city of Bryansk over the Desna River. It went straight through. The next day he was wounded again, and we next saw each other at the medical battalion. Pyatnizki was lying on a high pile of cushions. His condition was serious. Two days after my wounding I was taken to a hospital in the rear area, which is how I became separated from Pyatnizki. When I read the account about Pyotr Pyatnizki, I thought that it was about our Pyatnizki. He was so brave and determined.

Apparently the soldier wounded on the Desna in 1943 was only a namesake of Pyatnizki. But the publisher was right. They were similar in many ways: fighting spirit, courage and bravery. And these qualities described all our soldiers.

We were not expected in Severez, but the secretary of the district committee, an understanding man, put a car at our disposal. We drove a 100km on difficult roads, crossed a large field, came past a low shrubbery and then reached Severez. We stopped in front of a house in which Jevdokiya Pyatnizkaya lived. But she was not at home. She was at work, and her son too.

And then she came towards us, wearing a thickly wrapped shawl and short dress. Her heifer, which had been grazing on the riverside, had gone off on its own. She was agitated, she knew why we were there, but did not know who we were.

Then the village committee chairman pushed in between us. 'Who are you then?' he asked and checked our passes.

Pyatnizki's house was small. It had three windows and a Russian stove. As we entered, the picture between the windows caught my attention, and I looked at it closely. A reproduction of the Reichstag. The building had been photographed from the side of the Spree. Tanks and guns stood next to the smoke-blackened walls. A red flag glowed in a window on the second storey.

There are the pillars, there the broad area where Pyatnizki fell, hit by a bullet.

She is very reserved. 'If you see Kolya – he looks like Pyotr. He is the father as if cut out of the picture.'

When the Kolchos [collective farm] was founded, Pyotr was still only half a child, an orphan. Together with his brother, he was one of the first in the Kolchos. He was given the horses to look after. He was not big, but sturdy and broad-shouldered.

Pyotr Nikolayevitch enlisted in the first month of the war. His son, Nikolai, was born soon afterwards. Mail did not arrive for a long time and he was already assumed to be dead, but one day in winter the post woman stood on the doorstep. Pyotr wrote: 'I know that I have a son, but I just do not know what he looks like.'

I recounted to Pyotr's fellow countrymen, who had sat down on a log outside the house, how we had fought for the Reichstag.

A picture of Pyotr Pyatnizki hangs in the Kletno school. Before I drove to the school I looked out the head of the tractor brigade.

'Lads, is Nikolai Pyatnizki among you?'

A blonde lad stepped forward. I introduced myself and explained the reason for my visit. The head of the tractor brigade came up to us. He was a comrade of Nikolai's father. He was prepared to give Nikolai one or two days off so that he could come with us.

We were shown a briefcase at the school. It contained Pyatnizki's biography, documents and newspaper cuttings. The children had collected them.

It was already getting dark. The route went through the woods. We were on our way again.

A marsh began and the road worsened. I thought – nothing vanishes without a trace, nothing will be forgotten – the homeland will retain everything in its memory.

CHAPTER THIRTY-TWO

An Heroic Russian Warrior

I had the opportunity of driving to the Kuban, to the towns where I had lived before the war and where my mother was buried. On the way I made a stop in Rostov on the Don. I wanted to see the city and stay just a day, and although I stayed longer, I saw neither much of the city nor of the Don.

As soon as I had checked into a room in the hotel, and put down my bag and my document case with my unfinished manuscript, I sat down at the table in my overcoat and picked up the telephone to call the farming equipment factory.

'Call the foundry', said someone.

I telephoned and was told that the shift had already ended. I explained to the girl at the other end of the line that I had come from Moscow and was only in the city for one day. Apparently this was convincing. After a short time I heard a deep voice: 'Yes, please?'

An hour later I met him in my room. He was wearing a knitted shirt with an open neck and sailcloth shoes.

This was Berest, the deputy political officer from Neustroyev's battalion. Berest, the negotiator who, dressed as a colonel, went into the cellars under the Reichstag to persuade the Germans to surrender. His battalion commander, Neustroyev, had accompanied him – Neustroyev as adjutant and the lanky Berest in his leather jacket.

And that is what he looks like today. I had not been able to recall his face, and he too could hardly recognize me again. What can one say? So much time had passed, I would not have recognized him on the street. He seemed much bigger to me.

Now we sat down together and chatted, discussed memories and argued a little. He had a good memory.

I did not stay in Rostov for just one day as I had intended, but two.

The next day Berest took me to work and we drove to a small housing estate that was not quite cut off from the ditch that supplied water. He lived here modestly in one room, having given up space to accommodate the family of a demobilized soldier.

Photographs hung on the walls of his room. One of them was of his father, who had the same strong stature as the son. The picture, taken during the First World War, showed his father in his military uniform and cap with a cockade. Another photograph was of his daughter, who resembled her brother.

When our unit was disbanded in Germany after the war, Berest had gone into the navy and had lived in Sevastopol. I had often been there without knowing this. Like everyone he had lived in the emergency accommodation on the northern side before the city had been rebuilt. Today he and his wife, a nurse, are proud of this time, and I understand them.

Suddenly I recalled a notice that had appeared in our division. On the day that the war was finally over I went to the mobile office from the Reichstag and wrote a notice for the next edition of our newspaper: 'Our units took the Reichstag by storm. Involved in this historical battle, Pyotr Schtscherbina, Nikolai Byk, Ivan Prygonov, Vassili Rednev, Kusma Gussev, Kantara and Yegorov won undying fame. This operation was led by the valiant hero, Captain Stepan Neustroyev.'

We had laughed a lot about the 'Hero', as Neustroyev was small and thin. An overzealous writer had added this word, the rank of captain being too simple for him.

Now I was sitting with Berest, who really had the stature of a hero. Much was said, much not said, but when we had to take leave of each other, Berest took me to a taxi rank. There were several people waiting in front of us. Five or six excited lads were arguing, the dispute threatening to come to blows.

'Now, now, take it easy', said Berest.

The pugnacious lad looked round at him. When he saw Berest he fell silent.

A car drew near. We shook hands once more.

CHAPTER THIRTY-THREE

Resurrection

'Few know', so ran an inscription in my notebook, 'that the Komsomolz Danilov participated in the fighting for Berlin. As his company came to the street leading to the Reichstag, he hoisted the Red Flag on the corner of a building. Pyotr Danilov died a hero's death.'

This appeared in an account published on the anniversary. One month passed, a second, and I embarked on a long-planned journey. I drove via Rostov to the Kuban. In Krasnodar I visited a Kolchos on one of those hot harvest days. Then I called home from the hotel.

'Pyotr Danilov is alive! Your Danilov is alive!' I heard my wife say. 'Tass is asking whether you had known Danilov personally. He is now living in the Sverdlovsk area. A letter has come for you about it.'

I replied that this was wonderful news. But I had not got the information to hand.

Two weeks later, as I was in Minvody, where my route had taken me, my room-mate told me about the case. He was an old man, a former engineer. He was apparently deaf to all that concerned the war. He was due to retire and wanted to go to the Kuibyshev area to plant vegetables and learn how to take photographs.

But there was no one else there that I could open up my heart to, and so I talked to him. He listened to me with half an ear. Apparently he did not see why he should talk to me. Finally he said: 'I believe that I heard about it on the radio. When would that have been? Then I read about it.' And then he added that he had read about it in the *Stavropoler Pravda*.

'Has he been here long?'

'Ach, the article was very short!'

I asked him to be kind and, if it was not too difficult for him, to look for the article. He went with me to the library, which was next to our room. The librarian brought the relevant file. He flicked through and found what we were looking for. In the fourth column a note had been printed. It bore the title 'A Hero of the Reichstag is Alive'.

My sentence about Danilov was cited and it went on: 'When the inhabitants of Byngi village, near the town of Nevjansk in the Urals, read these lines in "Pravda", they will think: could this be about our Pyotr Stepanovitch?'

And then the newspaper reached the hands of Pyotr Stepanovitch Danilov, the stocky, thoughtful man with a sunburnt, weather-hardened face. He was just over 40, the article added.

'Yes, it is about me', said Danilov after a while and recounted details about the battle for the Reichstag.

> Metre by metre our company pressed through the cellars of destroyed buildings to the Reichstag. We needed days to do it. When we finally reached the street from where the Reichstag was visible, our Lieutenant Falenkov hurled himself forward with the flag. He was killed immediately. Then I picked up the flag and ran with my comrades to the next building. Some time later I came to the hospital.

The doctors saved the soldier's life, but he returned home as an invalid. Pyotr was unable to return to his trade as an electrician. Then he collected water in water bottles for the soldiers fighting for the Reichstag. This was very expensive water, as at any moment a bullet could have killed him.

Before the war he had been passionately interested in hunting, the Taiga and the behaviour of the animals, and decided to become a professional hunter.

Soon afterwards he had received a packet of letters from home, including one bearing the stamp *Stavropoler Pravda*. It was signed 'L. Gavrish', who wrote:

> Your publication has roused a lively interest among the Stav-ropolers, among whom there are many who took part in the storming of the Reichstag. The assistant stoker at the Red Metal Worker factory, Ivan Savelyevitch Gristshenko, remembers you and the now widely known Pyotr Danilov.
>
> Ivan Savelyevitch tells how he and two other soldiers carried Danilov out of the fire. Your notebook surely also contains these names.

There followed the address of I.S. Gristshenko, who lived in the village of Michailovskoye.

Next day I called Lidia Ivanovna Gawrish. She explained that Gristshenko remembered me from when I visited him in the regiment and had taken notes.

'Really?'

'You were allegedly with a Konsomol organization. He said that you were large and had the rank of a Lieutenant Colonel.' I promised to search for details in my notebooks, but said that I had little hope of finding anything relevant. I had already found the most interesting thing – Danilov was alive, he was alive and well.

Later I leafed through page after page, interested only in the names. And there I found the name Danilov! Guards Lieutenant Petersherski, Nikolai Petrovitch had told me about him. Consequently I had not been confused, I had not made an error.

Could I assume from such publications that they were all alive, could I go to the right places to find them?

Like this Danilov, who even believed his company commander to be dead, could I also bring others back to life that had actually fallen? Then Clarion Ivanovitch from Tsherkassy would get his son back, Lyuda Sumenkov her father, battalion commander in our division who fell in the Kalinin area, also Falenkov.

A letter awaited me at home in Moscow, from the pensioner W. Rybin from Nevyansk. In it Rybin reported firstly that he had met Danilov with pupils of the Byngier School and that he had spoken of his experiences. He had been badly wounded. Medical orderlies had found him and taken him to a dressing station. He had lost an eye.

The letter contained a photograph of a man in his forties. With his gaunt face and field blouse he still looked like a soldier.

CHAPTER THIRTY-FOUR

In Childhood, in Early Childhood

We had a number of these youngsters. There were some in every regiment, sometimes even in every company. I did not get to know all of them. There were some interesting lads among them – for example, in the regimental reconnaissance platoon.

I had unfortunately forgotten the name of that lad. Now, meeting front comrades, we remembered it. One said the boy had grown up in Vovka and came from the area of Staraya Russa, another claimed that the boy was called Shorka.

We found him on a photograph. He was standing with soldiers on the walls of the Reichstag, wearing a short field blouse and his cap pulled down over his ears.

Many of these youngsters were war orphans who had attached themselves to the troops. There were forty-three in the regiment in which he then served, himself a boy. He was very young. He had been brought up in the Kalinin area. He had been sitting in front of a burnt-out house, and the soldiers did not know where they should leave him. There were no relatives. We entrusted him to the partisans.

Wherever we fought, wherever we went through, through the Kalinin area or Beloruss, everywhere there were children without a roof over their heads, homeless children. They got accustomed to the soldiers and the army, and were at home with the divisions. Our orphans did not remain behind, they came to Berlin, coping with the problems like all the others on the march. They did not have an easy time.

We had decided to let him learn to be a compositor and had taken him on in the regiment. But I seldom saw him there with the composing stick. Mishka had neither pleasure in nor inclination for composition. Thus his hands and his nose, especially his nose, were always smudged. It was as if he worked with his nose, sticking it into the composing box.

Mishka had white blonde hair. Even his brows were whitish. That is perhaps how he came by the nickname 'Lead Dust'.

If Mishka was on to a good thing, his eyes turned blue. But when he was annoyed they turned dark.

I have forgotten his surname. We always called him Mishka and he addressed us as 'Comrade Lieutenant', 'Comrade Captain'. No one especially concerned themselves with him and no one was clear what Mishka should be doing. He did not even know himself.

Before Mishka came to us he had already been with other units, in the divisional bakery and also with the head of supplies. Mishka behaved badly. He found it difficult to subordinate himself, and we were certainly poor teachers, needing to be taught ourselves.

Mishka was not spoilt. When he perceived that I was sympathetic to him, he was sorry and moved over to my dugout.

'Can I be your orderly?' he asked and brought some hot tea. Then he brought the food in two mess tins. In one of them was gruel, in the other soup. He placed the containers on the small, roughly fashioned table. He pushed my papers aside and we began to eat. Mishka had a good appetite.

At the table Mishka complained about his fate. He lived here in day-time, had nothing to do and the captain complained about him. And he had not been given felt boots.

Mishka liked to grumble. He praised his former chief, a Major Stepanenko in the Intelligence Company. He had seen to it that he also got food and a new uniform.

I knew that our captain did not just complain about him. He was also very hard on us and often we grown-ups waited for a smile or some praise from the captain. But I did not tell Mishka that. I wanted to be polite and defend the captain. I told Mishka that he was himself responsible for his trouble and his misfortune because he did not learn and did not want to learn. He had nothing to complain about the food and the felt boots.

During chats like this Mishka usually mentioned a Petka, who allegedly had had more luck. Petka had ended up in an artillery regiment and was already a gun-layer, having received specialist training.

I knew no Petka and doubted his existence. Apparently he was a figment of the imagination. But Mishka tried to convince me. He and Petka came from the same village. When they were liberated, they had both joined an army unit together. Nevertheless Mishka had gone to an artillery unit. But he had specifically wanted to be a signaller – though cable drums are so heavy!

I listened to his prattle and eventually said: 'You are a little lazy-bones, Mishka!'

Mishka wasn't really a lazy-bones, He just couldn't tolerate being ignored. If one praised Mishka then he hacked wood with enthusiasm, filled the lamps with oil and almost burst with energy.

The best work for him was heating the stove. One could not hold him back. He had even acquired a saw and now sawed the wood when it was needed.

While I was browsing through my articles and reporting acts of heroism, Mishka made the fire and I usually only noticed when it began to crackle. Then Mishka would raise his head and look at me.

Mishka was uncouth and discontented. We called him a child of war. Among us soldiers he often felt himself superfluous, but he was only a child and it was more difficult for him.

Mishka was a farmer's boy. Once we took up quarters in a small farmhouse. There was a farmer's wife, a child and even a calf. Here Mishka was happy and began rocking the child. But he had to be sent to the supply depot to collect rations. Had he not gone there, he would have had to work at typesetting, and he did not want to do that. So he preferred to carry tinned food and groats.

In his childlike imagination Mishka believed that war was more interesting. Everything bored him. He had assumed that he would be given a horse or a gun, but he had to wash the cooking pots and crank the vehicle.

Here we published a newspaper, and wrote steadfastly, although there was a war on. He tramped from one dugout to another, getting wet feet. Somewhere there was firing, but he saw nothing. He moaned and I failed to understand him. Really, why did he not learn anything?

But what did I really want from him? Above all, had he gone to school, and if so, for how long? It seemed to me that he had only attended three classes.

Mishka spoke little of his home and seldom. I believed that his mother or an aunt were alive. He received letters from his village and wrote himself to someone. I best remember the letter that he had received from a friend and showed me. This youngster had been drawn into the war with Mishka, but had gone to another unit and even to another front.

When we spoke frankly with each other again, Mishka gave me – I fully understood what a great show of confidence this was – a letter from his friend to read. It was a long letter.

'How are you? I am well', wrote his friend, who seemed to be very different to Mishka. 'My unit liberated Kiev. Soon, dear Mishka, I will be promoted to corporal. And then it is not far from becoming a general.' Perhaps the joke about the general came from the writer himself, perhaps he was only repeating the words of an adult.

Then followed reminiscences about their home village and his parents' house. And he concluded: 'Do you know, Mishka, how we as children, walked with the girls?'

I folded up the letter and gave it back to Mishka. 'A good letter', I said. 'Write back to him.'

Mishka beamed. He was pleased that his friend praised him and had written him such a clever letter.

Ah, boys, boys, for you too the peaceful days were already long gone; I too was already in the second year of war ... as a child!

That same day I understood how our Mishka viewed life.

Our long discussion came to an end and busy day-to-day life took over. Somehow Mishka vanished from my thoughts as a new editor joined us who needed my advice.

What became of Mishka I do not know, either he was longer with us or I do not remember any longer. It could also be that he was sent home. Perhaps there was an order issued as we marched into Polish territory that all these youngsters were sent to their homes in the rear area.

But Shorka was in Berlin. The soldiers of the reconnaissance platoon, to which he was assigned, took care of him. During the fighting the youngster had to stay with the baggage. As soon as it became a little quieter Shorka appeared with the field kitchen.

The scouts sewed him a uniform, even the cap and his cross-belt fitted him properly.

It is quite possible that Mishka was in Berlin like Shorka, that he was with another unit at the same time that we found ourselves there and went along the same streets.

While I am writing this I have everything in front of me – the spoiled Shorka, our restless Mishka and also his friend, the 'General Corporal'. I see them all, and it is as if time has stood still, as if they were then in the foxholes on some snow-covered fields in the long field blouses not tailored for them, in the heavy half furs and men's shortened over-coats, these children involved in the great war.

Meanwhile they have grown up and become adults, these children. If they were then 10 years old and we, their commanders and superiors, often only 20, then they must already be over 30 now.

What could have become of them?

I would like to meet up with at least one of them.

CHAPTER THIRTY-FIVE

Marisia

I am 20 years old. We are in a liberated village in Poland. Little Marisia has climbed up on my knee. She looks at me. As I bend down to her and nod, she is happy and smiles at me.

The mother of the child, slim and young, looks at me and looks at her daughter. Then, with mixed Polish and Russian, Pani Helena asks me where I come from.

'From Siberia.'

'Siberia?' she asks in astonishment. 'My God! A quite different world!'

Helena does not move from the oven. She is not as busy as she pretends. I sense that I am sympathetic towards her. At lunch she talks to me about herself and her life. She tells me how Marisia was frightened of another soldier who recently lived here. When the little one saw him in the yard she would run into the room. 'Mama, Mama, the German!'

I let Marisia ride on my knee. She is delighted. Then I recite the words of a children's song to her. Astonishingly clear and with great enthusiasm, she says after me: 'Cockerel, cockerel Goldcomb …'.

Marisia smiles, I smile – we are both delighted that she learns the little song so quickly.

Helena looks at us. Then she goes outside and comes back with an armful of hay.

For Marisia, who is already rubbing her eyes, it is long time to go to sleep. She slips down from my knees, but Helena takes care to lay her down. I hear nothing more of them. I grope my way to the bed allotted to me and fall asleep before Marisia.

CHAPTER THIRTY-SIX

Our Little Friend

We had another young orphan lad in our battalion. At that time we were fighting in the upper reaches of the Volga. The youngster was about 8 years old. In time he would become a real man.

For the time being we knew that our unit would shortly be going into battle. Such things became clear. Committees appeared, the ammunition was replenished, everyone receiving one or two packets of biscuits.

When the regimental commander saw the youngster, he flew into a rage. He was right, it was not the time to be concerned with children. He ordered him to be handed over to the local organizations immediately.

We were very fond of him but could not take him into battle with us. We had to break up during the night. We handed over the youngster to the village Soviet, whose chairman promised to look after him.

Our battalion commander took the separation very much to heart. Furiously, angrily, he went about shouting at everyone who crossed his path and grumbled at us all.

We marched almost without a break for 60km, stopping in a wood late at night. In the morning when our cook went to the stove to cook the porridge, he found the rascal curled up in the pot sound asleep.

The cook decided only to tell the sergeant major for the moment. They both agreed to hide the boy. While he was in the pot nobody knew about it. The cook asserted that the scamp must have already hidden himself before we set off.

Everything then went smoothly. Everything went as it should. Our battalion commander was surprised when he saw him. But he too acted as if he had forgotten the village and its chairman with whom he had spoken himself. The sergeant major gave orders that the youngster was not to be seen by the colonel.

So the youngster, a sturdy lad, stayed with us . He got on with the soldiers and as long as the war lasted shared shelter, food and the stores in the dugout.

CHAPTER THIRTY-SEVEN

Pavlov's House

I did not go to Stalingrad during the war, but I remember well that we often asked if Pavlov's house was still holding out.

How often we heard about it in 1942 and 1943! The Soviet information reports also mentioned Pavlov's house and its steadfast defenders regularly. When the defence ended and the Fascist troops surrendered, one kept on writing about it.

The house stood on the city boundary half destroyed, but the soldiers established themselves there, defending it with incomparable heroism. The Fascists did not advance one step in this sector.

The garrison of this house fought for two months, only a few of them surviving. From the beginning they were led by a sergeant. I do not know his forename, but his family name was Pavlov. Everyone referred to him as Pavlov, his forename was never mentioned.

After the war I heard from someone that knew Pavlov well. Until then Pavlov had worked as the secretary of a departmental committee.

We kept on fighting after the battle on the Volga. Throughout 1943, 1944 and then part of 1945. Then we reached Berlin. How long ago had been the fight for this city that at that time called itself Stalingrad!

And then after the victory one of our regiments assembled in Berlin. A general who had taken part in the fighting on the Volga bend – I have forgotten his name – examined the first rank and stopped in front of a soldier. He was a soldier like any other. His padded jacket was shrunken and his cap had acquired a reddish sheen. He did not look young any more. Four braids bore witness to his wounds, of which three had been severe. One does not meet such a man as this every day, and even less at the end of the war. So it was no wonder that the general stopped in front of this soldier. He asked: 'Stalingrader?'

'Yes, Comrade General! Stalingrader!'

The general scrutinized him. 'Wounded four times?'

'Yes, comrade General, four times.'

The general considered. Why didn't the soldier have any decorations?

He looked at his adjutant as if he was to blame, was quiet for a while and turned back to the soldier. 'What is your name?'

'Pavlov, Comrade General.'

'Pavlov?', the general laughed, 'Pavlov!' the name obviously appealed to him.

'Are you the Pavlov who defended a building for two months?' The general smiled and the soldier naturally too. 'Have you heard of him?'

'Yes, I am he.'

'What?' said the general. 'That cannot be!'

The soldier was silent.

'Then you are a hero!' said the general. 'Where have you been up till now? Where are your medals?'

'I have none', replied the soldier.

The general turned to his adjutant, looking at his breast for a long time, then suddenly took the star from his own jacket. 'That is yours!' he said, fastening the medal and embracing and kissing the soldier.

That was how Sergeant Pavlov, the defender of the Pavlov House, unexpectedly received a decoration in a Berlin street at the end of the war.

One can naturally have doubts about this story. I myself have had reservations because, as has already been said, much was written about Pavlov's House and about Pavlov. I repeat that I do not know if everything happened like this and if the story is true. It is probably a legend.

Perhaps it was actually another incident and then Pavlov was ascribed to it. Incredible stories are concocted about people like this, but even if the story is made up, it is worth recounting.

At the time the Volga–Don Canal was opened I was in Volgograd. The city baffled me. I had expected something very different. It was mid-summer and there were very high temperatures for the two or three days we were there.

We went down some smoothly finished steps to the Volga. We were then on an island that was already protected by enormous trees – lindens or elms, we could not distinguish them in the darkness. We trudged between the unusually high trees and sank deeply into the sand. In fact I had expected something else.

Our men had held the steep bank, which dominated here. The foremost line of defence had been the bank. 'There is no land beyond the Volga!' Now I could understand this saying. There was really no means of withdrawing. Behind them had been the Volga. Chests on the bank, legs in the water was how one could describe it.

Where previously the trenches had run are now pedestals capped with tank turrets, and on the pedestals we found the inscription 'The front line ran here'.

There were no such towers at that time, only soldiers in their trenches, just a few soldiers in every company sector. I asked locals where Chuikov's headquarters had been. 'On the river bank', 'over there' and they showed me the dugout that had been made right over the water in the weak, crumbly bank.

We found the last remaining ruins in the centre of Stalingrad. Several streets had already been rebuilt, even the pavements had been asphalted. Only here and there hung projecting reinforcing props and rusting balconies.

Characteristic of the street noise was the sound of building machines, noises I knew from Sevastopol.

In the department store we saw the door that Paulus had been led out of. A sales assistant showed us the cellar in which Paulus had sat.

Our hotel lay in the city centre not far from the planetarium being built and the Square of Fallen Heroes, where the son of Dolores Ibarruri and Cholsunov, a pilot who had defended Madrid, is buried.

I asked the way to Pavlov's House. Some did not know where it was, others asserted that it was some distance.

One day before our departure we set out to look for it. We came through a bright, wide street in which there were new houses. It was the Street of Peace. We asked what the street had been called previously, but nobody knew. Then we turned down a lane, and edged through under cranes, around equipment and over clay and chalk.

We came across a young man spattered with chalk and carrying a bucket. 'Can you please tell us where Pavlov's House is?'

The young man stopped still, looked at us, took the bucket in his other hand and said: 'Come, I will show it to you.'

The young man looked at us surreptitiously as he came alongside us. 'Who are you then? Why are you looking for the house?' he asked

I explained that I was not from here, yesterday I had been at the Volga–Don Canal and today I had simply wished to see Pavlov's House, as did my wife, who had fallen a little behind being unable to keep up with our pace.

'I thought that you were Pavlov', he said.

'No, I am not Pavlov', I replied.

'I have recently been asked several times where Pavlov's House was', went on the builder. 'I have been looking for it. I recognize nothing any more, everything has changed so much.'

'Have you been here already several times then?'

'Yes, I am myself Pavlov', he replied.

Now I followed him to the house. It appeared that he had gone past it without recognizing it. 'We were there', said the young man.

Shirts, blouses and washing were hanging on lines. In front of us was a four-storeyed, medium-sized house. It stood not far from the Volga between other buildings. It was a quite normal housing block. The neighbouring buildings all looked new, being bigger and taller. They had pushed back this unassuming, often re-plastered and long-occupied house.

The young builder's labourer took up his bucket and moved off, while we looked at the building. Half of it was already whitewashed. Only part of it was still black. The holes had been cemented in.

'Was it badly damaged?', I asked.

A painter replied, 'Oh, it had hole after hole like a sieve.'

We went to the corner and read on a noticeboard raised to the height of the second floor:

Pavlov's House. Prominent Defence Bastion. This building was from September to November 1942 defended heroically by a group of soldiers from the 13th Guards Rifle Division under the command of Sergeant Pavlov.

CHAPTER THIRTY-EIGHT

Vitali

I had first got to know Riga after the war. I saw the towers and turrets, the grass-grown embankment, the cathedrals and churches of the old town, the Latvian soldiers' cemetery.

I was in a building bounded by a narrow street and a wide green square, the Museum for Latvian and Russian Art. On the left in the museum is the Latvian art department and on the right the Russian. I looked at both departments. I examined the modern Latvian sculpture and pictures and also the masters of the last century. There was a lot, a great deal in this museum that I saw for the first time. With every step and turn I encountered a rarity, an unknown study of Ivanov's, then a splendid Levitan, I also found a portrait painted by Perov of which I had not been aware of previously.

It is a good museum. It possesses, although it is small, only the best and most valuable. A pity that I could not look round in peace!

Mainly paintings were exhibited, but in the corners and between the windows one could marvel at all sorts of sculptures. In the first room I noticed a small marble head, the bust of a young woman with a thoughtful face. Her delicate, clean countenance harmonized wonderfully with the pure marble. I could not take my eyes off her for a long time.

I must confess that I looked at her only fleetingly at first and went past without stopping but, once I had seen the whole museum, I went back to her. Next I looked at her from the window and saw her face in pale sunlight, then from the room in shadow. There I found the stone shining through and I had the impression that a warm light was coming from inside it. There was a scratch above one cheek and a bit had been broken off the nose.

The custodian of the museum was a big-eyed, gaunt woman with short black hair. We chatted with her and discovered that a lot had been lost during the war and much damaged. Soon after the end of the war a man in a soldier's greatcoat and a grey civilian hat appeared at the museum. He had stood here at the table. He had taken off his rucksack and started unfastening it. It had taken him some time to open the bag. The he pulled out an old field blouse, wiped the cover and she immediately recognized the sculpture. He had found it in a destroyed house in Berlin. The sculpture bore the name of the sculptor.

The soldier had enquired in many museums if the sculpture belonged to them. Finally he had discovered that it had been stolen from the Riga museum during the war.

CHAPTER THIRTY-NINE

Grandfather Olentshuk

He lived near me in Sivash and I wanted to visit him. But although I had intended to do so, I had not got round to it.

I cannot recall when I first heard of him. I was already aware of him as a small boy in the same way I knew of Budjonny.

Father had told us youngsters about him. Now we were grown up, were soldiers ourselves and Grandfather Olentshuk was still alive.

When Perekop was taken in 1920, Grandfather Olentshuk had led the Red Army over the Sivash, and Wrangel was driven from the Crimea at that time.

He had himself described the crossing at Frunse. I even remember the picture: Ivan Ivanovitch Olentshuk, who had led our troops a second time across the Sivash, was living where he had always lived. So it was not far to him – a laughable ten to twelve hours journey. An old friend of mine drove me to him.

Olentshuk lived in Stroganovka on the other side of the Sivash. He lived alone. Nothing hung on the walls of his house other than old furs, so modest was this old man. He had twice led our army over the Sivash, the first time in the Civil War, then in the Great Fatherland War. Then I had seen him. I was going along the street in Simferopol. It was summer and very hot. A man with a stick in his hand came towards me. I stopped short. But that, that must be Grandfather Olentshuk!

I had recognized him immediately by his beard. He was wearing a little cap and shoes of untanned leather on his feet. Under his jacket, or padded jacket – I cannot remember which – he had an old field blouse. Olentshuk had the swaying walk of a fisherman, which was unknown in Simferopol.

Gratefully I looked around me. He had already gone. So I had seen him by chance, Later I asked around and discovered that Olentshuk was in Simferopol visiting a friend.

Grandfather Olentshuk died several years ago.

CHAPTER FORTY

Tales of Captivity

Much time has passed and I have forgotten many things. It must have been in Pomerania, as soon afterwards the Oder offensive began.

I was put in a field hospital, but did not stay long. A certain foreboding made me feel that the offensive, the last move, could begin at any moment, and the objective this time was Berlin.

We were lying in a small room, a large number of patients with a variety of complaints, heart problems, soldiers with ulcers, and burns. One had lost his eyesight. We lay in four bunkbeds in our small but warm and sunny room. I lay underneath, the most agreeable place.

I did not feel better than many, but not as bad as the seriously ill. Naturally I had my notebook with me as usual. It was under the pillow and I kept on pulling it out.

The building in which we were accommodated was of medium size and stood in a busy street. When the vehicles drove past it swayed and shook. At night the headlights shone on the walls and touched the patients, those sleeping and those awake, who were turning to and fro with the pain and inability to sleep.

I wrote poems here. The war events were not often reflected in them, for they were poems, such as one can even write in wartime, about people separated from each other.

Opposite me on the upper bunk was a very young lad, younger than all the rest of us, and we were all young then. He had a husky, croaky voice. At times his breathing was difficult and red flecks appeared on his cheeks. Everyone knew what that meant.

Our only way of passing the time was talking to each other. Whole days were needed for this. We came from various units and even the longest-serving were different. One of them had fought since the first day of the war and another had recently come to the front. The young lad opposite me wrapped himself in silence, but listened attentively and somehow cheerfully, although he seemed to be a reserved person.

When I awoke one morning, I felt much better. The tank soldier with the burns, who lay so close to me that I constantly feared knocking him, was groaning less. His head was completely bandaged up.

The sun was shining into the room.

That lad was soon awake too and writing in a book. Like me he stuffed his book under his pillow when the porridge was brought round. A poet, I thought. A few days later I held his book in my hands. That evening he read his poems to us, which were very similar to our own. Silence reigned in the room. The men, who had suffered incredible privations in the trenches and some wounded as many as seven times, listened in silence.

With moving, touching words the young lad related how he had been hunted by dogs, how the police had beaten him. He told of the barbed wire surrounding the camp, where he was given nothing to eat or to drink and not allowed to sleep at all.

In 1941 he had been taken off to Germany. He had spent three years abroad and had been in many camps. Coughing, he recounted how once some of our soldiers were delivered to the camp that had been established on Osel Island. This opened up a side of the war that we had not heard about until now. We lay silent and motionless, even the badly wounded tank soldier near me.

We heard how in November, stripped down to their belts, they had had to remove tree trunks from the icy water of a river. The dead had been fastened crosswise on the cart and buried hastily in deep ditches in the woods.

The worst thing was the hunger. The prisoners got a mug of watery soup. Often one of them died before he reached the cauldron.

The youngster came from the Smolensk area and was called Vassili Vassilevski. Until his liberation he had been in a camp near Schneidemuhl. As our troops approached the town he had fled from the camp with a comrade. They had hidden themselves for a whole week in a cold barn before our scouts arrived.

When I was released, Vassili remained in the hospital. I do not know where he went then.

I had the impression that his days were numbered and do not know what happened to Vassili, what his destiny was. I do not know whether he was able to take a weapon into his hands again and to march into Berlin as he had dreamed.

And nevertheless, as I set about writing about him I decided to use his name and not to alter it. Perhaps he has – as I very much wish – remained alive.

CHAPTER FORTY-ONE

We are Going On!

I looked at him and was unable to work out whom he resembled. Few photographs of him had been published and they did not all present his face in the same way. He was still flying and he was the only person who had seen how the sky looked above him and how the earth looked from the universe.

Yuri Gagarin.

When I got home my wife told me that she had heard his voice. He had already landed. A report had already been made from the landing place. Then the report from space was repeated on the radio. I pressed my ear to the loudspeaker but was not able to understand everything. There was a lot of background noise, probably because of the speed and motion.

'Everything went well, everything worked normally', assured the cosmonaut. 'The equipment worked normally, everything was normal ... everything was good, everything in order. We will go on.'

Yes, that is what he said: 'We are going on!'

At first I was puzzled. Perhaps he is not alone, I thought.

But he said once more: 'Everything in order. All worked normally. We are going on.'

So had the days as the end of the war came closer, as the Reichstag got nearer, our commanders in Berlin reported by line and radio: 'That and that point have been reached, I am at such and such a place ... we are going on!'

Those days had much in common with those today for me, the same excitement and the same gleam in the eyes.

Without our victory then, this fresh start today would not have happened.